The Complete

Power of Attorney Guide

for Consumers and Small Businesses:

Everything You Need to Know
Explained Simply

By Linda C. Ashar, Attorney at Law

Author of *101 Ways to Score Higher on Your LSAT* and
The Complete Guide to Planning Your Estate series

THE COMPLETE POWER OF ATTORNEY GUIDE FOR CONSUMERS AND SMALL BUSINESSES: EVERYTHING YOU NEED TO KNOW EXPLAINED SIMPLY

Copyright © 2010 Atlantic Publishing Group, Inc.
1405 SW 6th Avenue • Ocala, Florida 34471 • Phone 800-814-1132 • Fax 352-622-1875
Web site: www.atlantic-pub.com • E-mail: sales@atlantic-pub.com
SAN Number: 268-1250

Library of Congress Cataloging-in-Publication Data

Ashar, Linda C., 1947-
  The complete power of attorney guide for consumers and small businesses : everything you need to know explained simply / by Linda C. Ashar.
      p. cm.
  Includes bibliographical references and index.
  ISBN-13: 978-1-60138-311-2 (alk. paper)
  ISBN-10: 1-60138-311-8 (alk. paper)
  1. Power of attorney--United States--Popular works. I. Title.
  KF1347.A97 2010
  346.7302'9--dc22
                              2009052280

Printed in the United States

PROJECT MANAGER: Melissa Peterson • mpeterson@atlantic-pub.com
FINAL EDITOR: Chris Kissell
PEER REVIEWER: Marilee Griffin • mgriffin@atlantic-pub.com
INTERIOR DESIGN: Samantha Martin • smartin@atlantic-pub.com
ASSISTANT EDITOR: Angela Pham • apham@atlantic-pub.com
FRONT & BACK COVER DESIGN: Jackie Miller • sullmill@charter.net

Printed on Recycled Paper

We recently lost our beloved pet "Bear," who was not only our best and dearest friend but also the "Vice President of Sunshine" here at Atlantic Publishing. He did not receive a salary but worked tirelessly 24 hours a day to please his parents. Bear was a rescue dog that turned around and showered myself, my wife, Sherri, his grandparents Jean, Bob, and Nancy, and every person and animal he met (maybe not rabbits) with friendship and love. He made a lot of people smile every day.

We wanted you to know that a portion of the profits of this book will be donated to The Humane Society of the United States. *–Douglas & Sherri Brown*

The human-animal bond is as old as human history. We cherish our animal companions for their unconditional affection and acceptance. We feel a thrill when we glimpse wild creatures in their natural habitat or in our own backyard.

Unfortunately, the human-animal bond has at times been weakened. Humans have exploited some animal species to the point of extinction.

The Humane Society of the United States makes a difference in the lives of animals here at home and worldwide. The HSUS is dedicated to creating a world where our relationship with animals is guided by compassion. We seek a truly humane society in which animals are respected for their intrinsic value, and where the human-animal bond is strong.

Want to help animals? We have plenty of suggestions. Adopt a pet from a local shelter, join The Humane Society and be a part of our work to help companion animals and wildlife. You will be funding our educational, legislative, investigative and outreach projects in the U.S. and across the globe.

Or perhaps you'd like to make a memorial donation in honor of a pet, friend or relative? You can through our Kindred Spirits program. And if you'd like to contribute in a more structured way, our Planned Giving Office has suggestions about estate planning, annuities, and even gifts of stock that avoid capital gains taxes.

Maybe you have land that you would like to preserve as a lasting habitat for wildlife. Our Wildlife Land Trust can help you. Perhaps the land you want to share is a backyard— that's enough. Our Urban Wildlife Sanctuary Program will show you how to create a habitat for your wild neighbors.

So you see, it's easy to help animals. And The HSUS is here to help.

THE HUMANE SOCIETY OF THE UNITED STATES.

2100 L Street NW • Washington, DC 20037 • 202-452-1100
www.hsus.org

Dedication

To my mother, who has steadfastly encouraged me in all things

Table of Contents

Preface   **15**

Introduction   **25**

Chapter 1: What is a Power of Attorney?   **31**
An Overview of POAs 32

Chapter 2: Types of Powers of Attorney   **37**
Childcare POA..38

Health Care POA..39

Financial POA 42

    All-in-one POA 43

    Durable and limited/unlimited POAs.................... 44

Statutory Forms 45

Chapter 3: How to Choose an Attorney-in-Fact (or Agent)   47

Responsibilities of the Attorney-in-Fact 52

You as the Agent 56

Having the Conversation 57

Know what you want and why you want it 58

Location 59

Body language 60

Conversation skills 61

Overcoming communication problems 62

Explaining Your Choice to Others 66

Chapter 4: Childcare Power of Attorney   71

Your Commitment in a Childcare POA 72

Limited/Limited Nondurable POA for Childcare 73

Chapter 5: Financial Power of Attorney   75

General Power of Attorney 78

Limited Power of Attorney 78

Unlimited Power of Attorney 79

Limited POA for real estate.. 80

Durable Unlimited Power of Attorney 81

Selecting a Financial Attorney-in-Fact 82

Chapter 6: Medical and Health Care POA   87

Noteworthy Right-to-Die Cases...89

Karen Ann Quinlan 89

Nancy Cruzan 90

Terri Schiavo.. 91

The Aftermath..96

Impact of the Quinlan, Cruzan, and Schiavo Cases..........97

Durable Health Care or Medical POA 100

Choosing an Attorney-in-Fact for Health Care................101

Living Wills..102

What is Right for You?...103

Important terms and concepts to know 104

How to Make a Decision...115

Consult your physician 116

Chapter 7: Other Documents to Consider in Addition to Your POA   119

Affidavit of Attorney-in-Fact...120

Revocation of POA...121

Forms Relating to Health Care POAs 122

    Living will 123

    DNR order... 125

    Anatomical gift form 126

    Living trust.. 129

    Revocable living trust.. 132

    Last will and testament 133

This Is A Lot Of Work — Do I Really Need To Worry? 137

    You cannot afford to die... 138

Chapter 8: Working with an Attorney to Prepare Your POA   141

Locating an Attorney 142

Working with the Attorney..143

Making Sure the Relationship Works.....................................145

Firing an Attorney..147

Chapter 9: Specific State Laws 149

Chapter 10: How to Research for Your State's POA Laws 165

Finding Additional Information 171

Why People Get it Wrong 171

Research is boring 172

People do not know what they want 172

Break the Spine 173

Take a holistic approach 174

Read between the lines 175

Chapter 11: Signing Your POA 177

Take it Seriously 177

The POA Signing Ritual 177

Conclusion 181

Appendix A: List of Power of Attorney Types 183

Appendix B: Sample POA and Estate Forms 185

Where to Find Blank Forms..187

General Power of Attorney..190

Revocation of Power of Attorney 198

North Carolina Statutory Short Form POA.........................198

Oklahoma Statutory Form for Power of Attorney............203

Durable General Power of Attorney Effective
at a Future Time (New York Springing POA)....................207

Advance Health Care Directive Form................................214

Power of Attorney for Health Care 217

Illinois Living Will Act (755 ILCS 35)................................224

Illinois Health Care Surrogate Act (755 ILCS 40)..............226

Illinois Power of Attorney Act (755 ILCS 45)....................227

Indiana Living Will Declaration...227

Indiana Life-Prolonging Procedures Declaration..............229

Statutory Living Will Form in North Carolina 230

Pennsylvania Advance Health Care
Declaration Statutory Form...238

Pennsylvania Out-of-Hospital
Do-Not-Resuscitate Order 241

VIRGINIA ADVANCE MEDICAL DIRECTIVE.................243

Appendix C: Estate Planning Worksheets   253

Your Estate in Black and White..259

Prioritization 262

Who, What, How, and When..263

Essential Documents and Accounts Inventory....................263

Party Planning with an Unusual Twist.................................283

Estate Plan Summary Sheet..286

Annual To-Do List...287

Estate Planning Quiz Answers..289

Glossary of Terms   293

Bibliography   301

Author Biography   307

Index   309

Author's Preface

This book surveys in an easy format the many uses and benefits of the legal device called a "power of attorney." Although the term is in reference to a document, the concept it represents is a much more compelling and important notion: that of one's ability to make decisions and sign documents as if he or she were another person — lawfully.

The concept of agency — one person acting for another — is as ancient as time. The use of an image, token, or document as a device to evidence a person's (the agent's) ability to speak and act in place of another (the principal) dates back to the first interactions between human groups. In ancient times, merchants, leaders, landowners, and rulers routinely dispatched agents with documents carrying their seal, thereby empowering the agent on their behalf for all manners of business transactions. For a broader assignment of powers, a king would give his trusted agent his ring bearing the royal seal to signify the agent's importance — his power to literally stand in for the king.

These delegations of power fulfilled the role intended by the legal mechanism called "power of attorney," in which the "attorney" is simply any person designated to transact business on behalf of another. The following is a documented, ancient example of the use of power of attorney in a combined business and family context:

Circa 562 B.C. in Mesopotamia, a man named Itti-nabu-balatu acted for his brother Bel-kishir with respect to their father's business. Both inherited rights to the business from their father, but the son Bel-kishir was not involved in the business. With Bel-kishir's power of attorney, the brother acted on his behalf in running the business and was obligated to deliver to Bel-kishir his proportionate share of the business proceeds on an ongoing basis. This power of attorney was sworn before an official, much like a notary, who affixed a seal to the document.

Under the ancient Babylonian and Assyrian law codes, a son living in his father's house was not permitted to contract, buy, sell, or give goods or coins on deposit for a transaction, unless he held his father's power of attorney empowering him to act for his father.

Generals and presidents also have had need of powers of attorney to assist in the conduct of their affairs at home. The following example, with the original held in the U.S. Library of Congress, is an example of one of many such powers of attorney executed by George Washington to enable the conduct of his personal affairs. This is an example of a power of attorney granted to a trusted agent for a limited purpose — that of representing Washington concerning specified real estate and related dealings:

*"I do by these presents constitute and appoint John Jameson Esq. of Cul-
peper County in Virginia to be my attorney for the purpose of representing my interest in the great dismal swamp. – and I do hereby authorize
& empower the said John Jameson to vote in my behalf, on all questions
which may come before the Dismal Swamp Company (of which I am a
member) at any of their meetings and to act for me in all things concerning the same to the best of his judgment as he would for himself, except
to sell or mortage the property – All which notes, acts & doings, legally
performed, shall be bindin on me. Given under my hand and seal in the
City of Philad. This 16h day of Feb'y – 1795."*

— George Washington

Washington authenticated this limited power of attorney by his
official seal.

Fast-forward nearly 100 years to Europe in 1892, when married
women in various countries were legally prohibited from own-
ing property in their own right. In Italy, though, at that time
a wife could act similarly to a single woman and manage her
own property if she possessed a general power of attorney from
her husband.

The authentication of powers of attorney has historically also been
done with witnesses and officials called notaries. Use of notaries
to authenticate documents — including documents authorizing
an agent's power of the principal — was an ancient practice that
augmented the legal or bureaucratic system, not so differently
from today. Notaries are older than Roman times, but they became important in the highly organized civil system of ancient
Rome, where they were called scribae or scribes. They were func-
tionaries of the Roman legal system, empowered to transcribe

and register public and private documents. A notary might have been utilized to assist in writing agency documents — or powers of attorney as they are now called — and authenticate them using their official notarial seal.

The use of notaries or similar officials to authenticate powers of attorney dates to the early days in American history as well. The following example of a notable power of attorney is from Green DeWitt's granting authority to James Kerr to establish a colony of settlers in the new State of Texas in 1825 and evidences the seal an "alcalde," on J. Norton. This power of attorney relates to a historic passing of land from Mexico to the new state of Texas. An "alcalde" would have been a mayor, magistrate, or perhaps the equivalent of a notary in a Spanish town.

Green DeWitt's Power of Attorney to James Kerr
14 July 1827, Old Station on the LaBaca

"Know all men by these presents that whereas, I, Green Dewitt, of the colony of my name, in the department of Texas, in the Mexican United States, did obtain a grant from the supreme government of the state of Coahuila and Texas, bearing date the 15th day of April, 1825, to settle four hundred families in the department aforesaid, and within certain described limits as willfully appear by reference being had to said grant. Now know ye that I, the said Green DeWitt, have made, constituted and appointed and by these presents do make, constitute and appoint James Kerr, of said department, my true and lawful agent and attorney in fact, for me and in my name as empresario of said grant, to do and perform all and singular the duties imposed on me, the said Green Dewitt, by virtue of said grant and the nature of my contract with the state aforesaid, in as complete and full a manner as I myself might or could do, were I do-

ing the same in person; and my name to use as his own, at his will and pleasure, touching these premises to carry into effect all legal proceedings by me made; to seal, execute and deliver such grants, deeds and conveyances and other instruments as might be fit and lawful for me to do under the colonization law, the instructions of the commissioner and political chief, and also of the state and general government; hereby ratifying and confirming and by these presents allowing whatsoever my said attorney shall in my name, lawfully do, or cause to be done in and about the premises, by virtue of these presents.

In witness whereunto I set my hand and seal, at the Lavaca Station, on this the 14th day of July, 1827, and the sixth year of Mexican independence. Green DeWitt (L.S.) Witnesses: Wm. J. Russell, Abram M. Clare.

The foregoing power of attorney was Signed, sealed, acknowledged and delivered by Green Dewitt and the subscribing witnesses in my presence, at the Lavaca Station, on this the 14th day of July, 1827. J. Norton Alcalde"

Note that Green DeWitt's power of attorney to James Kerr sets out expressly that Mr. Kerr has the power to act as "I myself might or could do, were I doing the same in person; and my name to use as his own, at his will and pleasure." This is the essence of a power of attorney and why its carrying an official seal is so important. Also, in addition to the alcalde's certification, it is attested by witnesses named Russell and Clare.

Today, notaries are used as adjuncts of the legal system to verify oaths and authenticity of documents. Considering the historical context of both delegation of agency powers and the role of notaries, it is not surprising that powers of attorney still flourish as important business and personal functions, and in most jurisdictions, documents require a notary's authentication to be recognized legal. Third parties to whom they are presented must have reason to believe in their authenticity, especially when the agent who presents the power of attorney is a stranger.

In the times before faxes, phones, e-mail, and the Internet, such papers and tokens were all the more critical; agents traveled long distances taking months, even years, to complete their travel circuits. Delegation of powers by agency was critical for doing business and for governments to hold onto the threads of control. In short, the carrying of the principal's "power" to act in his stead enabled commercial and military mobility and communication; ensured stability; and made money. Then, just as now, the trust placed in the agent was key. History and literature are replete with betrayals by such persons. Overall, though, the system worked. The principle of agency promoted the development of civilization.

The need and importance for proof of one's power to act for another are no less relevant in society today than they were in those ancient times. The fact that communications can now be instantaneous does not obviate the need to prove one person has the legal authority to act on behalf of another. Indeed, the very ease of such communications makes such evidence all the more important. Otherwise, in today's fluid society, it would be all too easy for an imposter to assert authority he or she does not have. This, after all, is the crux of one of the most troubling modern crimes: identify theft.

As with anything else that develops in the law over centuries and through many different legal systems, powers of attorney — though basic in concept — are not necessarily simple to devise, especially when defining a specific purpose, or to execute to be legally binding. The explanations and forms provided in this book are here to simplify this task.

In the context of the array of legal tools and transactions available, the power of attorney remains a straightforward device whose efficacy is often overlooked. This book provides a comprehensive overview and guideline for the execution and applications of powers of attorney both for business use and for personal matters.

The primary focus of the coverage here is an understanding of the various types of powers of attorney that can be employed to assist in today's legal and social environment. Despite the advances in technology, people still cannot be physically in two places at the same time. The power of attorney obviates the obstacles of time and distance. In ancient time, these obstacles were primarily of importance in business and political matters, just as they are today. In present times, though, the power of attorney presents an additional useful application for reasons not contemplated in ancient times: People live longer.

A lifespan in ancient times normally was good for two or three decades at best; exceptions to that average were just that — exceptions. Today, people live well into their 80s. Medical advances permit people to survive or live with diseases that were insurmountable even 100 years ago.

With longer lives and survivability in medical procedures, the medical durable power of attorney has become an important document for a person to have in place. Yet this key document in one's life planning is often overlooked or misunderstood. The considerations for implementing a medical durable power of attorney and the kinds of situations in which it can and should be used are explained in this book. Powers of attorney become void if the principal becomes mentally incompetent except for "durable" powers; those are expressly designed to continue in force in such situations. As well, alternative documents, such as living wills and advanced health care directives, may be put in place. These are explained in this book.

Because the power of attorney accords the appointed agency a great deal of legal responsibility, choosing that person is no casual matter. For this reason, a portion of this book is dedicated to considerations in selecting an agent to hold a person's power of attorney. Depending on the powers delineated in the power of attorney document, the agent is going to have a great deal of latitude — truly, power. With power comes the opportunity to abuse it — potentially, a power to steal, where the agent has the ability to sign away property and transfer money. Powers of attorney are not subject to court oversight or monitoring. It is a private delegation from the principal to the agent that will be used in transactions with third parties. Thus, the decision of whom to select as one's agent, the person holding the power, is not one to take lightly. For this reason also, the principal retains the right to revoke a power of attorney.

Because of the potential for abuse, each state has enacted laws dictating how a power of attorney must be legally executed to be recognized. Virtually all require witnesses and/or a notary attesting to the principal's signature to ensure the person granting the power of attorney is who he or she says they are. Many states have forms set up for powers of attorney, making their drafting and execution easy. Many states have adopted the Uniform Durable Power of Attorney Act. A survey of each state's coverage of power of attorney and an appendix of forms is included in this book to provide the reader tools for selecting and using powers of attorney appropriate to his or her situation or need.

Agents holding power of attorney who abuse their power are not immune from criminal prosecution. The agent carries what is called a fiduciary responsibility. Under the law, the breach of that duty carries consequences. Giving someone a power of attorney is not giving that person a gift of all one's possessions; it is simply a delegation of authority to act for the principal as the principal so desires. State and even federal laws recognize the possibility of abuse in such situations, particularly where a durable power of attorney over financial matters is involved. Some of the punishable crimes for an agent's converting the power to his or her own benefit include embezzlement, forgery, fraud, larceny, money laundering, theft, and exploitation.

Thus, a person who elects an agent to hold a power of attorney has protection from abuse under the law. Ideally, with the proper choice of agent, such protection will not be needed. The potential for abuse should not be deemed a bar to exercising such a useful instrument, however. Having a power of attorney in place to handle life's surprises is good advance planning.

This book is designed to assist in that advance planning and to ease the difficulty of determining how to handle transactions, emergencies, and other life circumstances that will inevitably accost anyone throughout life. Many such circumstances should be managed with the assistance of legal counsel. With the tools this book provides, decision-making will be easier, as will focusing upon the type of professional legal representation needed to finalize the appropriate powers of attorney and keep them updated.

Introduction

A power of attorney (POA) is an important legal document that can be useful in many situations in one's life. If you are reading this book, you may be wondering whether you need a POA. Before assuming you do not need one, ask yourself the following questions:

- Do you care about your family members?
- Do you have or plan on having children?
- Do you own property in more than one location?
- Do you expect to age?
- Could an accident or illness render you unable to handle medical, personal, or financial affairs?
- Would you ever travel out of the country and need to have personal or business matters handled for you in your absence?

If you answered "yes" to any of these questions, then a POA held by someone you trust can make life much easier. Do not worry if you find legal work or paperwork daunting or intimidating. This book explains how to acquire various types of POAs and use them to your advantage. An illustration along the way will be helpful.

MEET THE JONESES

Meet the Jones family. As you read this handbook, these people will help you focus on the importance and various uses of power of attorney.

Family patriarch George Jones, 57, is a construction manager. Diane, his wife of 25 years, is 56 and works for the phone company. They have two grown children, Jason and Kristin, both in their 20s.

Jason is married to Shelley, and they have a 3-year-old son, Alexander.

Kristin recently graduated from college and is embarking on a promising career selling pharmaceuticals.

This hypothetical family is representative of families across America. George and Diane have worked hard over the past quarter-century and built a nice nest egg. They try to be thrifty and have accumulated enough assets to look forward to a worry-free retirement.

Jason and Shelley enjoy being young, and neither has put much time into thinking about savings. They are busy discovering the world and prefer action to planning. Jason has a landscaping job, and Shelley works as a bank teller while setting up her own business on the side. Jason and Shelley's mutual love of volleyball, country music, and their baby boy occupy them during the weekends.

Kristin has always been a top achiever and is careful to plan everything in detail. Her well-designed strategies, attention to detail, and thorough execution have contributed to her business success.

As our tale unfolds, our hypothetical family will go through some trying times. It is a good thing they (and their troubles) are fictional, because they will suffer complicated situations in a shorter time period than most, for the purposes of illustration. However, thanks to statutes and legal precedent, everything will turn out all right in the end.

There are times in life when the unpredictable prevails, despite our best efforts to stay in control and on top of things. Outside events, the needs of others, our health, or good old Mother Nature may disrupt our plans at any time. We may not like to think about such disruptions, but it is important to be prepared.

Likewise, it can be stressful and scary to think about issues surrounding personal injury or the end of our lives. Many of us understandably avoid imagining what life would be like after a tragic accident, or what will be left behind when we die. Although thinking about such events can be emotionally taxing, preparation ultimately provides more relief than ignoring the possibilities would.

Fortunately, there are ways to lawfully enlist the aid of others to help us navigate these stressful situations. Our federal and state laws provide individuals and businesses with a tool to help ensure safe passage in challenging times: the power of attorney.

In essence, the POA is an understanding between you and another person you have selected to represent your interests. This person — also known as an "attorney in fact" or "agent" — acts alone on your behalf when you are unable to make necessary decisions for yourself, for whatever reason.. For these reasons, you must be sure you can trust the named attorney-in-fact before executing the document that hands over such power.

Sooner or later, most people who are in business, have valuable possessions, or wish to protect loved ones likely will encounter at least one of the following situations:

- Planning for a child's normal care

- Caring for a child with special needs
- Protecting personal wealth
- Expanding a business
- Caring for aging parents
- Dealing with health problems or accidents
- Purchasing a home
- Transferring property by sale or lease
- Using an agent to do taxes
- Planning for the well-being of a spouse or other family member if you are incapacitated
- Handling business matters from a distance while traveling
- Ensuring that a business will continue following your retirement
- Being in any situation or circumstance that requires the assistance of another person to act in your place

The POA is a recognized legal tool allowing you to maintain control over complex situations that naturally arise in the course of living, such as the ones listed above. The basic concepts relating to POAs are fairly simple, although there are variations, depending on the type of form required and differences in individual state laws.

In the past, many people automatically turned to an attorney for help with a POA. And it is true that in many cases, legal guidance is still necessary. Also, many people feel as though most legal issues are far too complicated to be handled on their own. Legal jargon can be intimidating and can feel like you need a law degree to get through it.

But when needs are fairly straightforward, it is possible and relatively easy to execute your own enforceable POA. Reading a guidebook such as this can help you avoid unnecessary legal fees. Many people need the protection offered by POA laws and involve a lawyer in what is often a simple process. POAs require witnesses and notarization, but depending on state laws, they are not always required to be recorded. In some states and situations, recording a POA could be required, especially relating to their uses connected with real estate transactions. In those states or circumstances requiring the recording of a POA with a court or governmental officer, legal assistance is always an option if you are not comfortable with recording it yourself, or are not sure of the recording requirements. However, if recording the POA is not a requirement in your state, you can avoid expensive legal fees by preparing your POA without assistance from an attorney. If you still feel that legal assistance is necessary, learning about the different types of POAs, their uses, and legal matters surrounding them before visiting the attorney can save you time at their legal offices, and thus save you money in the long run.

This handbook covers all the POA fundamentals and can be used as a resource for ready reference. You may read it from start to finish to gain an overall understanding of POAs, or use it as a pinpoint guide for specific types of POA documents. The inclusion of case studies from the field provides sample situations to help clarify the details and demystify the process.

The book begins with an introduction to the fundamental concepts of POAs and explains uses we normally have for them. Then, we will look at each type of POA in detail.

POAs work best when you choose an attorney-in-fact, or agent, whom you are confident about and also wisely choose successor or alternative agents. This handbook will help you make this crucial decision and explore the issues you should discuss with your representative(s) before you prepare the POA that gives them the power to make decisions on your behalf.

If you decide to obtain expert advice, the choice of legal counsel is crucial. A full chapter is devoted to making this important selection. We will also discuss forms, in addition to your POAs, that can help with similar medical, financial, and family-related decisions. To further assist you, this book includes a number of auxiliary tools, including sample forms, a list with individual state information, resources for obtaining forms, and other specific instructions. A glossary defines legal terms and other important words.

One last note: This book is intended as a guide for consumers, by consumers. The instructions contained herein are not meant as a substitute for legal advice. While there are basic principles, nuances of law can differ among states, and every person's circumstances are always unique. If you have any doubts or further questions regarding your needs and these guidelines, you should consult a licensed attorney about your specific situation.

Chapter 1

What is a Power of Attorney?

MEET THE JONESES

George Jones started a career in construction following graduation from high school. Eventually, George enrolled at a community college and studied project management. Being a project manager would allow him to work in a safer environment and to spend more time at home with his family. A gentle, intelligent man, George showed promise as a leader. A large local construction company hired him as a manager, and he has been working for the same organization ever since.

While George's life has unfolded with purpose and even joy, he has hit a few bumps this year. A serious dip in the housing industry has caused work to slow down, leaving George a little worried about maintaining the lifestyle to which he and Diane have grown accustomed. Due to the slump in new home purchases, work is slowing down for George's company. Prices for daily needs have skyrocketed, and George and Diane even canceled plans for a trip to Yellowstone, fearing the cost of gasoline would be too expensive. The rise in natural gas and electricity prices have made spending time at home more tense also, as the Joneses worry if they are using too much energy.

Meanwhile, Diane feels exhausted all the time, which causes George to worry. George is increasingly aware of his own aches and pains. Sometimes, especially on Sundays, George wants to do nothing more than sit in his easy chair all day. George and Diane both lament that when their grandson, Alexander, comes over, they cannot find the energy to play with him as much as they would like to.

An Overview of POAs

It may be helpful to note that originally, the word "attorney" applied to anyone appointed to represent another's interests. This is a broader definition than we use today, when "attorney" means a person with a thorough knowledge of the law, generally admitted to practice before a state bar. The concept of giving someone a POA (sometimes referred to as a "letter of attorney") recalls the earlier definition. A POA refers to the act of officially designating another person to make decisions and take actions on your behalf under specified circumstances.

The term "power of attorney" is used in a few ways. In the first instance, it refers to the legal document conferring the power of attorney. It is also used as a term of authority held by the person designated in the legal document; when that person acts on your behalf, he or she has power of attorney over affairs stated in the legal document.

You may also hear a POA called an "advance directive," which is a broader term referring to any statement — either spoken or written in a formal document — that clearly indicates a person's wishes for medical care should that person become unable to make his or her wishes known. The term "advance directive" refers to a health care or medical POA — or a POA document that specifically addresses medical concerns. In many states, an advance directive or advance health care directive has taken the place as the equivalent term for a living will.

When you complete a POA document, you are termed the "principal." The person you name in the POA to make decisions for you or to act on your behalf is titled your "attorney-in-fact" or "agent." In the case of documents pertaining to health care, this person also may be called your "proxy" or "surrogate."

Armed with this bit of vocabulary, you can go a long way in understanding what a POA is all about. For a variety of reasons, you will want the assistance of others as you proceed through your life. There will come a time when you may not be able to do for yourself and will need someone to help you. Most people want to ensure that their health and well-being — and that of their loved ones — are protected against unwarranted suffering or unnecessary complications. For some people, using a POA may be a calculated choice in their personal financial affairs, and they may implement one for convenience more than need. However, you do not need to be in the middle of a difficult situation to establish and use a POA. Setting up a POA before problems arise can make those problems much easier to handle.

The POA is a document meant to ensure smooth transactions with third parties. It is a way for your affairs to continue when you are incapacitated or otherwise unable to participate. The POA tells vendors, creditors, caregivers, and any other third party that you have given the person named in the POA permission to act in your stead. It is a security blanket that covers you during potentially difficult situations.

Many people encounter the need to have another individual represent their personal affairs under certain conditions. To do this with the full protection of the law, you must sign a POA stating your wishes and appointing a certain person as your representative.

If you do not officially assign responsibility for your affairs — whether financial or related to health care — to an attorney-in-fact through the appropriate document, a court will appoint someone else to take over in the event that you become incapacitated and cannot make decisions for yourself. Thus, the management of these personal and important areas of your life will become the responsibility of a court-appointed guardian, conservator, or committee. This appointment could take some time to implement, and the preceding will be public, as all court matters must be. The person appointed by the court may or may not share your beliefs, passions, or concerns and, thus, may or may not make a decision that you, your family, or your business partners will be happy with. You can avoid this by preparing your durable POA, living will, and/or advance directives in accordance with all legal standards.

While all 50 states and the District of Columbia have provisions for honoring POAs, the forms and requirements for legally preparing and executing a POA vary from state to state. Many states provide "statutory forms," or forms the legislature includes within the written law regarding POAs that are available for use within the state. Other states are less specific and allow for a variety of forms. The number of required witnesses and details of the notary's block in each state also vary. *See Chapter 9 for specific information regarding state laws.*

Aside from these variations, the process of creating and implementing a POA is fairly standard. The steps you will follow are:

1. Secure the proper forms or locate an attorney to assist. Use the chart in the appendix or individual chapters in this book to help you decide which form to use. *See Chapter 8 for more information about working with an attorney to prepare your POA.*

2. Confer in depth with your attorney-in-fact to ensure that person is fully informed and ready to take on the responsibility. *See Chapter 3 for more information on the relationship between yourself and your attorney-in-fact.*

3. Complete the form carefully, but do not sign it yet.

4. Assemble a notary and your witnesses, as required by state law, and sign the document in their presence.

5. Distribute copies of the document to creditors, vendors, doctors, and anyone else who may need this confirmation of the authority of your attorney-in-fact. Keep the original document in a safe place. In some states and for certain uses, POAs may be publicly filed with your court or other official in your county of residence.

Each of these steps is examined in detail as we proceed through this handbook. Our first question is, of course, what types of POAs are available, and in what circumstances are they needed? The next chapter presents the various types of documents that exist and how they are used.

CASE STUDY: IMPORTANT FACTS TO KNOW ABOUT PREPARING YOUR POA

Donna J. Jackson, Attorney at Law
PC President and Attorney
Oklahoma City, Oklahoma
www.donnajacksonlaw.net

Donna J. Jackson is a CPA and an attorney. She specializes in estate planning, including trusts, special needs trusts, wills, durable power of attorneys, living wills, taxes, probates, and business organizations, including corporations, limited partnerships and limited liability companies.

I recommend that every client should have a financial and health care power of attorney.

The greatest risk involved is selecting an attorney-in-fact who breaches his or her fiduciary duty to the client. The person named as having power of attorney should be someone whom the client trusts and who can carry out the wishes of the client. It should be someone who can take care of the needs of the client.

I recommend clients name at least a primary and contingent power of attorney so they will always have someone to make financial and medical decisions. If a client's family works together, it could be advisable to name co-power of attorneys.

I have used durable power of attorneys that contain both financial and health care powers. If the power of attorney will be held by the same person, it would be advisable to use an all-in-one power of attorney. I use separate power of attorneys in order to keep power of attorney from being too voluminous.

The agent with power of attorney should document all financial decisions and the money he or she spends on behalf of the client.

The power of attorney can be revoked by filing a revocation with the county clerk or recorder.

If the principal uses an attorney, the attorney should counsel the client regarding the client's choices. If the client names more than one power of attorney as co-trustee, there should be a tiebreaker procedure.

Chapter 2

Types of Powers of Attorney

MEET THE JONESES

Jason Jones, George and Diane's eldest child, married his high school sweetheart, Shelley. They quickly had a child, becoming parents when Jason and Shelley were just 23. The grandparents were thrilled with the new addition to the family and love spending time with the baby.

However, a shadow is beginning to creep across the family's happiness. George and Diane see tensions growing between Jason and Shelley. The young couple does not discuss this with their elders, and it seems they are trying to ignore it themselves. But George and Diane are worried.

Their other child, Kristin, causes them some concern as well. Although she seems to leap from success to larger success continually, George and Diane wish she would slow down enough to establish close relationships. She is always busy with her career and never stays long enough in one place to make close friends, much less a boyfriend. Kristin says she is not lonely; she is too busy and excited about the future. Eventually, she wants to own her own business.

Although it can be used for a variety of situations, the POA most often is applied in certain types of life circumstances, including the care of a minor (childcare POA) or incapacitated person (durable health care POA) and the administration of personal finances (financial POA).

This chapter examines all three of these situations, so you can gather an idea of how the attorney-in-fact concept works overall. In later chapters, we will look at each specific type of POA in detail.

Childcare POA

A childcare POA allows someone else to make decisions for your child in your absence — whether that absence is voluntary or due to an unfortunate event.

Many necessary services for children require parental consent. Parental agreement is required for medical treatment. A parent also needs to sign off on school registration, field trips, and other permissions.

A childcare POA makes sense when a child:

- Has special needs and attends a camp out of town.

- Vacations out of town, state, or country — away from his or her parents — with relatives or friends.

- Lives with a relative to establish residency for school.

- Is placed in another home to avoid the abuses of a dysfunctional parent.

- Attends a camp or treatment center to deal with disciplinary problems.

- Is sent to live with friends or relatives while parents work out their own personal or professional matters.

It is important to note that the POA for childcare does not automatically give the attorney-in-fact authority over all medical decisions for the child; it simply allows the caregiver to authorize medical treatment in emergencies while the child is in the care of the attorney-in-fact.

If for any reason a child is not living with his or her legal parent or guardian, completing the POA and naming an interim caregiver as attorney-in-fact protects the child and opens opportunities for him or her.

Health Care POA

A health care POA covers medical decisions that need to be made on your behalf should you become unable to give consent for a procedure to take place. It is usually called a durable health care POA, meaning that the POA will not lapse if you become mentally incapacitated.

For example, Angela, 20, was injured and left in a coma following a car accident. Doctors think an operation will help Angela recover, but they need the patient's consent to proceed with this procedure in a legal manner. Fortunately, Angela had previously completed a POA, naming her sister, Kelly, as attorney-in-fact. Kelly is intimate with Angela's preferences and can give the doctors legal permission to operate, based on her authority as Angela's representative.

This example shows how creating a durable health care POA is a good idea for anyone who has left the care of his or her parents. Accidents and unforeseen circumstances that require the assistance of an advocate can occur at any time, regardless of age.

Most health care POAs are completed by people at higher risk of incapacity, and not by people of a younger age. Many people who reach middle age start to reflect on the possibility of becoming mentally or physically incapacitated. Every state legislature provides guidelines for making a determination of when a person is physically or mentally incapacitated, and commonly, the law tends to err on the side of patient's rights and self-determination. A health care POA will specify standards for making any judgments of incapacity, including certification by one or two physicians.

Why is this an issue? The law provides for decision-making abilities regarding your personal health by those around you, even if you have not otherwise designated this responsibility. By law, a guardian, spouse, child, or parent may be authorized to make decisions regarding your personal health in the absence of a specific directive from you. Any one of these people may or may not be personalities you trust, or they may not perform the actions you would choose for yourself, and instead may act on their own wants. Creating a health care POA allows you to decide who will make these choices when you are unable to do so, thus bettering the chances that your personal wishes will be carried out regarding your medical treatment.

Moreover, laws and standards of medical ethics may require doctors to perform certain types of treatments in given situations if no specific directive is given by the patient. While incapacitated, you could be subject to medical procedures that you would reject when conscious. A health care POA protects your choices and your rights even when you are helpless and do not have the ability to make decisions for yourself.

It is important to note that a living will supersedes a health care POA in medical situations. The living will is an advance health care directive that states the principal's preferences regarding life-prolonging procedures should he or she fall into a permanent coma or vegetative state, or if he or she is in the late stages of a terminal illness. The principal makes these decisions in advance, and they do not require another person to be involved, unless you so choose. The living will is a document that is kept close to the person concerned, so it is readily available in case of emergencies.

Another document many people sign in this regard is a do-not-resuscitate (DNR) order. Though living wills and DNRs are not the prominent scope of this book, you should understand the differences between them and your health care POA. *See Chapter 7 to learn more about the relationship among all these instruments.*

Financial POA

A financial POA allows someone to commit your money or other assets in business decisions, purchases, or other transactions on your behalf. The following are three examples of how a financial POA can serve your interests:

1. Charles is the successful owner of several businesses who stays extremely busy. He hires managers carefully, selecting people he can trust. Charles signs POA documents, giving those managers authority to pay bills and write checks in his name. This enables his businesses to run smoothly in his absence.

2. Darren and Claire have been married for a few years. They want to prepare for a time when they may be unable to make financial decisions together. They also want to prevent their children from having to deal with the confusion or undue responsibility in the event of Darren or Claire's incapacity. They complete mutual POAs giving authority to one another over their respective financial affairs. If Darren becomes incapacitated, Claire will have the right and authority to act in his stead and vice versa.

3. Monique is a fashion designer. There is an important fashion show in Europe, but Monique is tied up with work for a major client. She sends her trusted assistant to be her proxy at the fashion show, signing what is known as a "limited POA" that assures all Monique's fashion suppliers and cohorts that her assistant is authorized to do transactions and sign agreements on her behalf for the duration

of the fashion show only. Limited POAs are prepared for specific circumstances or time spans.

The need to use a financial POA may arise due to personal incapacity, or it may be an ongoing need as a result of typical business dealings. If your physical presence is not possible, or perhaps not desirable, in completing a transaction, using a POA allows you to effectively be in two or more places at the same time.

All-in-one POA

Finally, an all-in-one power of attorney is sometimes available, allowing you to designate the same person as your attorney-in-fact for financial and also health care decisions. You may use this form if you are a resident of one of the following states:

Connecticut	Indiana
Kentucky	Louisiana
Missouri	New Jersey
New Mexico	Ohio
Pennsylvania	South Dakota
Utah	Washington
Wyoming	

Three of these states have *statutory* (legislated) all-in-one forms — Connecticut, Indiana, and New Mexico. In the others, forms are created according to statutory requirements, but specific forms are not mandated. In any case, you may reduce your administrative work by dealing with just one form, if that answers your needs.

Be careful when using an all-in-one form, though, because if your state recommends the use of a specific statutory POA form for naming your health care attorney-in-fact, it is advisable to execute that POA separately, because the all-in-one form may not include provisions for your end-of-life choices. Another approach is to execute a living will in addition to the other forms. Given the intensely personal nature of these health care decisions, you may wish to consult an attorney about adding these powers to a customized durable POA form. *See Chapter 9 for more information on statutory forms.*

An all-in-one POA names one person to serve as both your financial and your health care attorney-in-fact. This gives one person a lot of power over your affairs if he or she elects to use it. This is certainly an aspect to consider when determining whether you will use an all-in-one POA.

Nonetheless, an all-in-one POA can cut down on administrative fuss if your affairs are straightforward, your choice of attorney-in-fact is obvious, and you live in one of the states that allow this type of POA.

Durable and limited/unlimited POAs

At this point in our discussion, it is worth making an important distinction. The basic POA in its most simple form becomes ineffective upon the incapacity or death of the principal. Principals who want their POA to remain in effect in the event of incapacity must sign a durable POA. The example of Darren and Claire, the couple described above, is one instance in which the durable POA is appropriate.

On the other hand, Monique, the fashion designer, uses a form called a limited POA, which becomes invalid after a given length of time or occurrence of a specific event. The multi-business owner, Charles, will almost certainly utilize a general POA or an unlimited POA, designating his managers as his representatives, but it will not likely be durable.

An unlimited POA gives the attorney-in-fact authority over any and all of your financial transactions and contracts. The unlimited POA allows you to delegate specific duties to your attorney-in-fact, and as with the basic POA, it becomes ineffective upon the incapacity or death of the principal, following the guidelines for execution prescribed by state law.

Statutory Forms

Most states have adopted the "Uniform Power of Attorney Act," a standard form that can be used to establish your POA. In fact, only two have not. If you live in Louisiana or Illinois, you will not be able to use a standard form and will need to create your own.

However, if you live in any of the other states — including the District of Columbia or the U.S. Virgin Islands — and wish to enact a durable POA, you can obtain a copy of this form from your state government. Though this paperwork may contain language that sounds similar to language in other states' forms, be sure to use the form prescribed for your own state.

If your state does not have a standard durable POA form in its statutes, you may use the generic form included in this book's appendix. If you have concerns regarding the use of this standard form, contact an attorney familiar with establishing POAs.

You will find that with a statutory form, you will need to indicate which powers you are giving to your agent with a check mark or your initials next to the desired powers; or, you will need to cross out, check, or use your initials to show which powers you are not giving to your agent. This is an important distinction to note. In the first type of form (we will call it Type A), your agent will only have the powers that you specify with the appropriate marking. In the second type (we will call it Type B), your agent will have all the powers listed on the form except for the ones that you mark out with the appropriate marking. So make sure you understand which form you are using.

To Review:

There are three main categories under which a power of attorney may fall. Each of these types of POA will be discussed in detail in later chapters.

Health care: A durable health care POA can cover many medical decisions that need to be made on your behalf should you become unable to give consent for a procedure to take place.

Childcare: A childcare POA allows for some medical decisions to be made on behalf of your child if he or she is not living with you for whatever reason.

Financial: A financial POA allows for someone to make business decisions, purchases, or other decisions or deals with your money on your behalf, if you are not present.

Chapter 3

How to Choose an Attorney-in-Fact (or Agent)

MEET THE JONESES

George Jones, although not so far from retirement, decides to proactively engage the economic recession and slump in housing sales. Alan, an old friend whom George met when studying project management, lives 1,000 miles away, but the pair have kept in touch. Alan, who is experiencing similar doubts about the economy, has suggested he and George partner in a moonlighting venture. The two men would supervise the construction of a large vacation home located some distance from either man's home. They would need to alternate traveling to the site to do the work. It would be too much of a commitment for either one of them to do alone, but Alan suggests that together they could share the responsibilities and make some badly needed extra money.

George thinks it is an excellent idea and feels like he still has the energy for it, despite that fact that he would need to be away from home occasionally over the next year or so. Such a business venture would allow George and Diane breathing room with their finances, and they may be able to take that Yellowstone vacation they have been dreaming about.

Diane's health is still a question, though. She does not seem to be getting any worse, but she is not getting better, either. George, however, wonders

> wonders if Diane is simply slowing down as a natural part of the aging process. Her spirits are good, and she makes it to work every day; maybe there is not much to worry about. He and Diane have always shared a lot of laughs and prefer not to get too serious about things. George has not mentioned anything about his concerns yet, and Diane was never one to complain about anything.

While considerations about which POA form to use and how to properly execute the signing are important, once you decide to create a POA, another important decision involves choosing an attorney-in-fact. Also known as an agent, proxy, or surrogate, they all indicate the person to whom responsibilities are allocated within the POA document.

The attorney-in-fact is the person who represents you in matters specified in the POA. Unfortunately, choosing your attorney-in-fact is a bit more complicated than naming your child or best friend. There are several legal restrictions as to whom this person can be. By law, the person must be of a minimum adult age, which varies from state to state. In addition, several states have eligibility restrictions. For example, doctors and health care providers are often deemed ineligible, as are care-facility owners and employees.

Some states offer exceptions if a doctor, health care provider, or community care-facility operator is a relative. If this person is a relative by marriage, however, that person may not be able to be your attorney-in-fact if that marriage ends.

We all hope to be near home should the need arise to utilize your attorney-in-fact. But it is certainly possible that you may be in another state when the unexpected occurs. For this reason, it is a good idea to abide by state restrictions regarding the identity of your agent. Should you need to activate your POA while away from home, state law almost always specifically says that your out-of-state POA will be valid as long as it conforms to the present state's code.

One last note about your attorney-in-fact: Many states specify that this person may not also serve as the witness to your advance directive or health care POA signing.

All of these restrictions are designed to prevent conflicts of interest that would cast doubt on the ability of your agent to exercise the best judgment for your interests in your place. A physician serving as your attorney-in-fact may feel more or less comfortable with performing certain procedures, but the doctor needs to be able to evaluate and recommend medical procedures without competing nonmedical factors. If that person is your agent, he or she may end up making a decision based more on his or her own comfort level, or with compromised medical evaluation, than solely because of your specific wishes.

Also, doctors and other health care providers are often courted (or perceived to be) by pharmaceutical companies selling and promoting everything from specific drugs to certain pieces of medical equipment. Physicians do not want to be placed in questionable positions of appearance of impropriety over medical decisions that may appear to be subject to considerations other than your wishes. The attorney-in-fact must act from an unbiased place. These laws and restrictions make that more likely. *See Chapter 9 for more specific information regarding your state's restrictions.*

Outside these limitations, you can select anyone you wish to be your attorney-in-fact. The government cannot tell you whom you must appoint to be your attorney-in-fact. For example, the law does not require your spouse, parents (if you are no longer a minor), or children to be named as your attorney-in-fact. When making a choice, take the following factors into account:

- **Place of residence**. Will it be important for your attorney-in-fact to be located in a certain place? If you are completing a health care POA, will you feel more comfortable with someone who lives nearby? If an emergency happens, it may be easier for your agent to be closer to you. An attorney-in-fact for a health care POA who lives thousands of miles away may be of little use when a medical emergency strikes. A financial POA may require an agent who can represent you in a specific setting, or when your presence is not feasible. For senior citizens, this can be a difficult issue. Adult children may live far away, or retirement may have led older citizens to a quieter, smaller, more remote location. Because employees of care facilities are often not eligible to become a person's agent, it may be helpful to consider enlisting the help of a friend, minister, or neighbor. It is necessary that this person be reliable and able to arrive at a hospital, doctor's office, or other health care facility if the need arises.

- **Trust**. Whom can you trust? Designating someone as your attorney-in-fact is giving significant authority to that person over your person and possessions. The appointment may be valid only at a specific time, or only in a specific set of circumstances. It may also be ongoing. Whatever the details of your document, it is crucial that you are confident in the representative and believe that person will faithfully perform his or her duties.

It may or may not be appropriate to choose someone close to you to serve as an attorney-in-fact. Perhaps you wish to spare a loved one the ordeal of making such difficult decisions on your behalf, or perhaps your loved one does not want to be put in that position. When considering the appointment of your attorney-in-fact, it is important to keep their opinions and well-being in mind, as well as your own. However, your agent does need to be someone you fully trust, at least in terms of the particulars of the POA document. If there is no one you can identify who meets this basic requirement, it is better not to complete the POA at all.

- **Expertise**. You may want to consider the skills or expertise of the individual you choose to be you attorney-in-fact. Is he or she capable of performing the assignment? The person you appoint as your attorney-in-fact for financial matters needs to be well-versed in dealing with business and money transactions. A health care attorney-in-fact should be someone who is energetic, determined, and a good advocate. He or she should also be good at making decisions quickly while under stress or in less-than-ideal circumstances. The attorney-in-fact should be well-organized and a good communicator.

Like an employer looking at a potential employee, consider the agent in his or her totality. For example, someone you are considering may be good at communicating, but may not work well under pressure. Someone else may work well under pressure but drives others crazy with an inability to be organized.

An attorney-in-fact does not have to be a professional. He or she needs to be comfortable with financial matters but does not need to be an expert. Your agent for health care decisions does not need to have studied medicine; but it would be best if he or she has the emotional strength to be a support in emergencies and the self-confidence to question and engage with medical personnel in your best interests.

In addition to selecting an attorney-in-fact, it is important to name at least one alternative or successor agent, in case the attorney-in-fact is unable or unwilling to perform the specified duties when the time comes.

Responsibilities of the Attorney-in-Fact

The POA document specifies actions the attorney-in-fact may or may not take on your behalf. In all cases, the document transfers authority from you to another person under a certain set of circumstances and for certain purposes.

For example, a financial POA requires management and oversight of financial transactions. A health care POA requires decision-making about your medical treatment and care if you become incapable of making these decisions.

The attorney-in-fact named in your health care POA will be the one to communicate with medical personnel and represent your interests. He or she will also be the one to make decisions about treatments that require patient approval.

The attorney-in-fact named in your Financial POA will be the one authorized to invest, spend, contract, or sign as your representative, according to the particulars set out in the POA.

Similarly, other types of POAs are specific to the "powers" described in the POA itself. In all cases, the document transfers authority from you to another under a certain set of circumstances for certain purposes.

After deciding on an attorney-in-fact, talk with that person about taking on this responsibility; share your expectations. Discuss every detail you can foresee that may require your agent's participation. Your wishes should be made clear for all eventualities. Your chosen attorney-in-fact may be unwilling to take on the responsibility for a variety of reasons. You should respect their wishes and find someone who wants to carry out the job they have been enlisted for. You should never finalize a POA with someone who is hesitant about signing the form. You want your attorney-in-fact to be confident in their responsibilities to fully know you can trust them with the specific aspect of your life you have designated.

Of course, you will not be able to anticipate everything. Share your broad point of view and make sure the attorney-in-fact understands it and will abide by it. Considering specific situations will be helpful.

Attorneys-in-fact are not free to act in whatever way they deem best, but instead are charged with doing whatever you would do in a particular situation. For example, an agent in a financial POA has fiduciary responsibility, meaning he or she acts solely in your interest. Your health care attorney-in-fact may well be inclined to make different choices for their own personal interests, but must act according to your stated wishes when called upon in your behalf.

It is important to again emphasize here that your designated attorney-in-fact is not authorized to do anything other than what is specifically indicated in the POA document. If you appoint your business partner to be your attorney-in-fact for financial affairs, this does not give him or her any authority regarding your health care. And, if your sister is your agent for health care, she has absolutely no say over your finances.

By giving authority and responsibility to another person through a POA, you are not giving away all control. You can revoke an agent's privileges at any time, and may continue to perform actions and make decisions for yourself independently of the agent. You continue to retain your identity and authority in all your personal and business matters. Through the POA document, you are sharing those responsibilities with another, but you are still free to exercise whatever rights you had previously.

From time to time, there have been incidents where an attorney-in-fact betrays a principal, or even steals from or compromises the well-being of the principal. It is said that a POA is only as good as the agent. For this reason, it is important to use the utmost care when appointing an attorney-in-fact.

Note that it is certainly possible and popular to name the same person as your financial health care representative. This is fine, especially if you believe this person is your best choice in both cases. Be sure to name an alternative agent, though, as depending on one person to meet all your needs could be inadequate. Also, take note that if your spouse is your agent and an accident happens, it is possible that your spouse will be with you and suffer the same trauma. He or she may also be incapacitated. An alternative covers this risk.

If you have different people serving as attorneys-in-fact for financial and health care matters, be aware that though operating independently, these two agents may have knowledge of concerns in both areas. For example, a financial agent may need to peruse and pay medical charges, and a health care agent may need to be aware of a principal's financial resources as they relate to health insurance and Medicaid or Medicare status. The Health Insurance Portability and Accountability Act (HIPAA) form for access to and release of your medical records is included as part of both the durable financial POA and health care POA, giving your financial attorney-in-fact authority to access your medical files to record and pay bills, and your health care attorney-in-fact access to medical information to make decisions about your health care.

It is possible to name more than one attorney-in-fact, specifying that decision-making and actions occur through majority vote. However, a group is much more likely than an individual to stalemate over decisions. Moreover, suspicions arise when responsibility is divided, meaning directives could get lost in legal bickering. Nonetheless, such arrangements can be made, most often in family situations.

You as the Agent

We have spent a lot of time discussing how to choose someone to act as your agent. However, after having learned a bit more about how a POA works and why it is helpful, you may find that you are considering becoming someone else's attorney-in-fact, or perhaps you were recently named as an attorney-in-fact and simply wanted to learn more about the whole process.

This may be the case if you have aging parents and you are their only child, or the child who lives closest to them. You may have a business partner who is getting older or simply taking on too many responsibilities. Any of these scenarios — or others similar — may call for you to take the initiative and discuss with someone the possibility of becoming their agent.

Looking to and asking for the ability to take on a responsibility like this may seem selfish in some ways. You will gain power over part of a person's life, and others near you may see this move as a power grab. Remember: Being someone's agent does not grant you unlimited power over the person's affairs — there are safeguards to make sure people are protected. Some of these safeguards have already been discussed. For example, the law prevents a primary care physician from acting as a patient's attorney-in-fact. We will discuss other safeguards in later chapters. Asking to be someone's attorney-in-fact is more a sign that you are concerned about his or her affairs and that you want to make sure the principal is taken care of in the way he or she would choose should the occasion arise.

The truth is that almost everyone could benefit from having someone assigned to act as his or her agent. Obviously, the elderly, people with children, and people with financial assets to be protected will need a POA. But people who are not parents, are young, and may not be considered wealthy may still find benefits from using a POA. Everyone has his or her own health to consider. Accidents and tragedies happen, and if a POA is not in place, you may not be able determine what happens to you if you end up in the emergency room.

The following section will discuss communication skills you can use whether you are asking to act on someone's behalf as their agent or asking someone to act on your behalf as your agent.

Having the Conversation

Because discussing finances or our eventual death can be uncomfortable, it is not unusual to want to skim over unsavory details when asking someone to act as an attorney-in-fact. Discussing financial details or pondering your eventual death may be unsettling; however, it is imperative that you communicate clearly and effectively so both you and the attorney-in-fact are in agreement.

Chances are you will have this conversation with someone whom you know well and who cares about you, but you should still be professional and as clear as possible. Being unclear during this initial conversation may result in problems later in the POA process.

When planning your first meeting, choose a location that conveys professionalism. If you meet in your home, make sure it is tidy. There are good reasons to choose a location other than your home or personal office: Choosing a neutral location puts each of you on equal footing, which facilitates discussion of important issues.

Know what you want and why you want it

The first thing you will need to be clear about is what you want out of your attorney-in-fact. Explain your wishes and how you want the agent to carry them out.

If you are sick, do you want any new or potentially experimental procedures to be carried out on your behalf? Are there some procedures that you do not want? Is there a procedure that you want done first? If you are dealing with a business situation, are there certain lenders, bankers, or executives with whom you do not wish to do business? Are there certain amounts of money or certain pieces of property that you feel comfortable with someone else handling, but not others? If your children become hurt or injured, are there certain procedures that you do or do not wish to be performed on them?

Write down your desires. Ultimately, these terms will find their way into your POA document, but before approaching your chosen attorney-in-fact, you should be completely aware of what expectations you have for the relationship.

It is also important to know why you feel strongly about the things that you do. You may decide for or against some medical procedures based on religious or philosophical beliefs. Your business practices may be based on family tradition, long-standing loyalties, or personal preference. It is not necessary that your attorney-in-fact share these beliefs, but he or she should respect your beliefs and understand them. It is a good idea to also write down why you feel these are the right decisions for you.

Location

Though you may intend to have this conversation with someone you know well and with whom you feel friendly and comfortable, do not let the casualness of your relationship lead you to set up a casual conversation. This is an important step, and where you have this conversation can affect the eventual outcome as much as choosing who will serve as your attorney-in-fact.

Choose a location that conveys professionalism. If you do choose to use your home, this is not the time to get cozy on the couch and raise the question during a commercial break. Think of this encounter as a meeting with a business client. Even though your chosen attorney-in-fact may be a close family member or a business partner you have known for years, you are discussing important legal matters, and the seriousness of the conversation should be conveyed through the environment where you choose to have the discussion.

As mentioned earlier in this chapter, choosing a neutral location to have this conversation may make both of you feel more comfortable about asking and answering important questions. If you do choose a location other than your home or office, make sure it is a place where you will be assured some amount of privacy. You will be discussing personal information, and you may not want that information overheard by strangers.

Body language

Another key to conveying the seriousness of the conversation to your attorney-in-fact will be your body language. Experts say more than 50 percent of information communicated during a conversation is delivered without words. The way you hold your hands, your head, and your posture — and whether you make eye contact — will tell your potential attorney-in-fact just as much, if not more than, the actual words you use during this conversation. Do not ignore your body language. Doing so may damage your communication and prevent important points from getting across.

While an overview of body language may seem unnecessary, consider how uncomfortable having a conversation about future illnesses or death could possibly be. Suppose you are an aging parent, and you would like to discuss signing a health care POA with your adult child. For children — of any age — coming to terms with a parent's eventual death is one of the most uncomfortable, gut-wrenching considerations. Your effective body language can help to make this conversation easier by relaxing your listener and showing him or her that you are at ease with the subject.

So, while it may not seem as though body language has much to do with establishing a legal relationship with another person, remember that though a POA is just a piece of paper that happens to award someone certain rights, privileges, and responsibilities, you are entering into a legal relationship. And like in other relationships, communication is extremely important, and body language is a big part in that communication.

Hand position

You do not have to be a sign language interpreter for your hands to be busy speaking. Whether your fingers are crossed or uncrossed, if your palms are facing out or in, or if your hands are in your lap or moving freely, you are conveying a message that you may or may not intend to deliver. To communicate effectively and put your attorney-in-fact at ease, you should learn and practice the movements that unconsciously make people feel comfortable, including open and outward-facing palms, unclenched fingers, and uncrossed arms.

The head and face

The way you hold your head and where your eyes are directed will give your chosen attorney-in-fact unconscious clues as to how you really feel about doing business with him or her. A moderately paced head-nod offers encouragement to the person you are speaking to, as well. When having a serious conversation, eye contact is a natural way to show that you are listening and that you care about what they are saying. Giving your attorney-in-fact a sincere smile shows that you are at ease with the subject of the conversation and that you have trust in their ability to perform the duties associated with signing the POA.

Conversation skills

Using effective conversation skills when discussing future POA relationships with your chosen attorney-in-fact is extremely important to ensure you are being as clear as possible. Being unclear regarding your expectations of the relationship can result in confusion when the POA actually needs to be executed. Effective communication also enables your agent to ask pertinent questions at the beginning of the legal relationship. With effective communication, you can ensure that you are communicating exactly what you intend and that all your wishes are clear. Using effective communication skills can also ascertain that your chosen attorney-in-fact is comfortable with taking on the responsibilities associated with the relationship.

Poor conversation skills are often a matter of habit. If you are not consciously familiar with visibly expressing emotions or conveying personal information, having a conversation regarding your eventual death or the care of your children can be difficult if it evokes strong feelings.

Many experts say that fear is the main cause of poor communication. Many people do not effectively communicate their thoughts because they are nervous about expressing their opinions. To quell that fear, we often try to communicate less directly. Approaching someone about your need to prepare for unforeseen events requires you to put a lot of trust into that person. You may feel nervous that your chosen attorney-in-fact will think you are being over-prepared, or that they will not take the conversation as seriously as you would like.

Overcoming communication problems

If you recognize yourself in any of the above problems, do not worry; there are a few steps you can take to ensure an effective conversation with your chosen attorney-in-fact:

- **Understand your communication style**. Aggressive communicators often have strong emotions, such as anger and frustration. They may use off-putting hand gestures and body language. Aggressive communicators often find it difficult to communicate what they really want. In contrast, passive communicators often feel powerless and unable to fully get their messages across to listeners. They may fidget often and smile or nod to show agreement, even when they do not agree with what is being said. Assertive communicators know how to convey limits and expectations to others in their conversations. They value their own opinion as well as the opinions of others. Communicating assertively is the best method for communicating with your chosen attorney-in-fact. When dealing with important legal matters, expressing your opinions and clearly defining your expectations is a must.

- **Understand your agent's communication style**. Which of the previous styles does your attorney-in-fact fall into? By knowing how they communicate, you can be prepared for how they may react to your conversation and help to resolve issues before they begin. When conversing with a passive communicator, you should encourage this person to express their thoughts. When conversing with an aggressive communicator, you should be assertive so your opinions and point of view are not lost.

- **Talking the talk**. Make active choices regarding the way you communicate your message. Do the following to control your physical communication:

— **Listen to your own voice**. The pitch and speed of your voice can greatly affect how well you communicate. If your voice is too high and without strength behind it, you may sound unsure of yourself. If you have a naturally high-pitched or light voice, practice lowering your voice a bit when you speak. This will give you more of a presence and cause people to take you more seriously. If you speak too quickly, you may end up sounding nervous or displaying a lack of confidence. You may also cause important information to be missed as the words fly out of your mouth. Try recording yourself talking about your POA. When a person is trying to control certain emotions, his or her voice may change pitch. It is possible that as you discuss important issues like your health care and finances, and begin to entrust someone with personal information and intimate duties, you may feel emotions that you did not expect, and the pitch of your voice may rise as you try to keep those emotions in check.

— **Look at your presentation**. You should have sample documents ready to show your chosen attorney-in-fact. You should have specific expectations ready to present to your potential agent. You should have research to back you up in case your surrogate has questions that he or she would like to ask. Make sure you have all the information that you need — all the information you would like to have if someone were asking you to take on this responsibility. The more prepared you are when you present this information to your agent, the more confidence you will show — and the more effective this transaction will be for both of you.

— **Say what you mean**. Determine exactly what you want and share this with your agent very specifically. There is no reason to be ashamed or embarrassed by your wants or needs. It is your money, your health, or your child; these are all important factors in your life, and you should feel free to speak frankly about them. If you are being evasive or somewhat dishonest about what you want, it is possible this will read in your face, body language, or tone. If your agent feels you are being dishonest, he or she may be less willing to help you in the capacity you would like.

— **Ask questions**. The best and most direct way to find out how your conversation partner feels, or what he or she is thinking, is to simply ask questions. Ask direct and specific, open-ended questions that allow your agent to discuss what they are thinking, instead of simply answering "yes" or "no." When you ask questions, do not be afraid of the answers. You may find that your agent does have questions or concerns. Ask questions with a spirit of truly wanting to know and understand what the other person is feeling or thinking. Conflicts are solvable, and it is helpful to learn to invite constructive conflict instead of trying to prevent helpful conversations from happening.

Explaining Your Choice to Others

The conversation you have with your potential attorney-in-fact will likely be a positive one. Yes, you are asking someone you care about to take on a certain amount of responsibility, and you will be talking about potentially emotional issues such as money, illness, and death. But you are also expressing to that person — by virtue of asking them to enter into this relationship with you — that you trust him or her and appreciate his or her relationship to you.

It will be beneficial for the people around you to know that you have prepared a POA and know whom you have chosen as your attorney-in-fact in case the need for execution of the POA arises. However, loved ones not chosen to represent you may be hurt because they were not asked to take on this responsibility. Similarly, if you own a small business and any number of employees or board members were up for the position of attorney-in-fact, there may be some hard feelings around the office. Or, if you come from a large family and have many children, siblings, or other relatives who may have been in the running to handle a health care POA, one or more family members may be jealous that you did not choose them.

Consider discussing the terms of the POA with those closest to you so there is no issue should a business deal or medical emergency arrive. The last thing you want is to have people confused, surprised, or conflicted about who is in charge when it is time to make an important decision. An open and honest conversation with these individuals will ease potential tension later.

The communication skills discussed earlier will certainly help you when it is time to tell expectant family members or business associates that someone else has been chosen to act as your attorney-in-fact. Using confident body language, understanding the other person's emotional point of view, and displaying effective conversation skills will assist you in having this conversation. The following are specific details for having this discussion with someone not chosen as your attorney-in-fact.

- **Do it soon**. In a family or workplace, news — both good and bad — can travel fast. It can be hurtful for someone not chosen to find out indirectly through the grapevine.

- **Get right to the point**. Though you want to be friendly and conversational, you also do not want to spend too much time before you let the person know what it is that you have to say. You can lead into the conversation by saying something like "Jason, I wanted to talk to you about my POA decision for next quarter." Then let the person know that the decision has been cast otherwise.

- **Use facts, and not feelings, to justify your point of view**. Let those around you know you have taken the time to carefully consider your options and decided to choose your attorney-in-fact based on a combination of the trust you have in that person, their expertise, and other needs, like location. Though you do not need to explain everything to the people who are going to be acting on your behalf as your agent, you should have solid facts at the ready in case they have any questions.

- **Do not just talk — listen**. Though you are the one with the news to deliver, do not forget to listen to what is being said to you, as well. Remember: Your agent may or may not always be able to perform his or her duties for you, and you may need to call upon one of these people in the future. Plus, you are all working together or existing as part of the same family, so ultimately, you are all working toward the same goals.

To Review:

Choosing your attorney-in-fact is a big decision. There are many factors to consider, and you should spend some time thinking about how these factors fit together and how they fit your needs.

Some of these factors are legal matters. The government cannot tell you who should be your agent, but it can tell you who is prohibited from being your agent. These restrictions are in place to avoid conflicts of interest and generally prohibit your own doctor, health care provider, or administrator at your residential care facility from acting as your attorney-in-fact. These restrictions may be lifted if the person who fits the above descriptions is a family member by blood or marriage. You should check with your state's laws to find out exactly how these rules and regulations apply to you. Other factors to consider include the location of your attorney-in-fact, your level of trust in the attorney-in-fact, and the level of expertise of your attorney-in-fact.

You may also determine that someone close to you needs an agent to act on his or her behalf. Aging parents and business partners are prime candidates for this. If that is the case, you may want to have a conversation with that person suggesting that he or she allows someone to act on their behalf in a POA relationship.

After you decide whom your attorney-in-fact will be, you will need to have a conversation with that person to explain his or her duties and to make sure he or she understands what is expected. Having serious conversations can be stressful for both you and your attorney-in-fact, and brushing up on your conversation skills is a good way to make sure your needs are clear, and any questions your potential agent may have get answered. Not communicating clearly may cause serious problems later if you and your agent are not in agreement as to what is expected in regard to the POA.

It is important to inform those closest to you that you have decided to prepare a POA and share whom you have chosen as your attorney-in-fact. You may also find yourself telling others that they were not chosen as your attorney-in-fact. If you are owner of a business with several managers or a part of a large family, those closest to you may have been expecting to be chosen as your attorney-in-fact. If this is the case, you will need to tactfully let the others who were wondering know the news. Using basic communication skills as well as specific tactics for delivering difficult news can make this conversation much easier. It will be important to let others know that the responsibilities of the attorney-in-fact have been assigned so that in an emergency situation, everyone will be able to act accordingly.

Chapter 4

Childcare Power of Attorney

MEET THE JONESES

In order to try to work out their marital situation, young parents Jason and Shelley have decided they need some alone time. They have decided to take an extended vacation out of state and would like George and Diane to watch their son, Alexander.

Because Jason and Shelley will be out of state for at least a few weeks, George and Diane are worried about meeting the needs of Alexander should an emergency arise while his parents are not around.

A friend suggested to Diane that the family set up a childcare power of attorney while Jason and Shelley are away. This would allow Diane and George to make decisions for Alexander regarding his health or education while his parents are gone.

Diane does a bit of Internet research and determines the family can set up the power of attorney without the council of an attorney. Diane, George, Jason, and Shelley prepare the power of attorney, and each party signs the document. Jason and Shelley head off on their vacation in comfort knowing that Alexander's needs will be met should an emergency come up.

A childcare power of attorney allows another party to make certain decisions on your behalf for the care of your child. These decisions are generally limited to emergency decisions when the child is out of your care for an extended period of time.

The person acting as your agent does not have legal guardianship over your son or daughter; he or she simply has the right to make certain decisions for that child if you cannot be reached.

Your Commitment in a Childcare POA

Generally, a childcare POA says you consent to certain details regarding the care of your child while the child is not living with you.

In a childcare POA, the agent may have the ability to give or deny consent for the following:

- Emergency medical treatment
- Extensive medical treatment like a surgery or hospital stay
- Actions that will help keep the child safe, such as providing a place to stay or leaving the child in the care of another adult
- Educational opportunities such as school or scholarship enrollment
- Disciplinary treatments — either by the agent's decision or at the discretion of another adult caretaker, such as a teacher or principal

A childcare POA involves both a child and an adult. Take time to select someone your child trusts. If you feel the best person to be your child's agent is someone he or she does not know, introduce or re-introduce the two to each other and explain how the POA situation will work. Give your child time to ask questions and to learn to trust the agent.

Before selecting an agent, consider whether or not the person works well with children. People sometimes feel anxiety when it comes to children — especially children who are not theirs. Maybe your agent is someone who makes stressful decisions quickly and confidently. Someone who is knowledgeable and knows how to handle himself or herself in a crisis is not necessarily comfortable making these decisions around or for a child. Spend some time talking to your childcare POA agent to determine if this person will be able to act in a confident and assured manner when dealing with a potentially panicking young person.

Limited/Limited Nondurable POA for Childcare

Unless otherwise specified, a limited POA for childcare states exact dates when the document is valid. This type of POA is often a helpful document to put in place if your child will be living with another adult for a defined period of time. In addition, a limited POA for childcare can be useful if you are unavailable when schools, camps, doctors, and other providers require a parent's signature before attending to your child's needs.

When using a POA for childcare, you are in no way abdicating responsibility for your child or giving up your status as a parent. Instead, you are giving the adult with whom your child is staying the legal ability to provide normal nurturing experiences for your child. The document allows for your agent to authorize emergency medical assistance only.

Do not confuse this temporary protection for your child with the complications of guardianship. A guardian is court-appointed through a complex and lengthy process and must report to the court. The duties of your childcare attorney-in-fact are simply to parent faithfully in your stead for a stated period of time.

The limited nondurable POA for childcare is essentially the same as the limited POA for childcare with one significant difference: The nondurable version becomes ineffective if you become disabled or incompetent, even if the child is still living away from you when the accident, injury, or sudden, debilitating illness occurs. At this time, the POA is automatically revoked, and the agent no longer has the ability to make the decisions outlined in the POA for your child.

To Review:

A childcare POA allows your agent to make certain decisions for your child in your absence. You may wish to appoint someone as attorney-in-fact for your childcare POA if your children are going to be living away from you for an extended period of time. This type of POA gives your agent certain powers, like the ability to make emergency medical decisions or allow your child to undergo certain medical treatments.

Chapter 5

Financial Power of Attorney

MEET THE JONESES

George Jones and his long-distance friend Alan agree to set up a loose partnership for the purpose of overseeing the construction of the vacation home. They will deal with a large number of vendors as they gather materials for the construction, and they will have to obtain licenses and inspections. They will also need to prove to vendors and officials that either one of them alone can make deals for both; George needs to be able to take action on details without his partner's being there, and the same goes for his partner when George is absent.

Diane admires her husband's resourcefulness and wants to help in this effort, as it will benefit the whole family. Diane enjoys surfing the Internet and knows she can find information about legal protections for the kind of deal on which George and his friend are embarking. While searching for pointers on partnerships, long-distance business techniques, and business legal matters, she learns about power of attorney. After careful discussion, George and Diane decide to ask Alan to agree to a power of attorney. Each man will sign a document granting power of attorney privileges to one another for the purpose of the home construction. They also agree that this is a process they can easily do on their own, without going through the expense of hiring a lawyer.

Interestingly, George and Diane's go-getter daughter has also encountered a need for a power of attorney. Kristen's employer has asked her to represent the company's interests in Ethiopia. She will be going there to live next month. Her parents are very worried and comforted only by the fact that this is just a year-long assignment. Her company signs a POA naming Kristin as attorney-in-fact regarding the company's concerns in the foreign country. The promotion is huge for Kristin, and she is bursting with excitement — but she is also wise enough to think about precautions that might be necessary, given the unusual nature of her assignment.

A financial POA allows an agent to represent you in financial matters. These may include the purchase of items, property, investments, or banking transactions.

The original idea for POAs came from the world of business and finance, in which enlisting the aid of a trusted representative can be exceptionally handy. The use of POAs for health care and childcare is a more recent development.

Financial POAs are used for many reasons. You might use one for such matters as:

- Banking and investing transactions
- Business transactions
- Real estate
- Legal affairs
- Investing
- Entering into a contract
- Operating a business
- Preparing for eventual retirement or incapacity

CASE STUDY: USING A LIMITED POA

Julie Inmon
Los Angeles

When my husband got a job in California, he moved away a few months before I did. I stayed behind in Texas so I could get our home ready to sell, finish up a project at work, and find a buyer for an investment property we had purchased together (the paperwork for this property was in both our names).

Once we finally had an offer on the investment property, we used a limited POA to allow me to complete the sale paperwork on our behalf, since my husband was not around to sign for himself.

The limited POA allowed me to sign in this specific instance but prevented me from signing for him in any matter other than what was specified on the POA.

I am not sure whether we could have just faxed the closing documents to my husband and had him sign a copy; I know laws vary from state to state on that sort of thing. But this made it much simpler in the event of a minor change or error in the documents. I could just sign the new copies, rather than having to go to Kinko's or my husband's workplace to fax them back and forth to California each time — which would have been especially troublesome, since there is a time-zone difference.

When using a POA, be sure you understand it. Consider a limited POA so you know the scope of it and do not inadvertently give someone more control than you intend.

A financial POA allows someone to make financial decisions on your behalf and sign documents in your stead. The POA may grant the agent authority over one specific transaction, certain types of transactions, or all types of transaction. The POA may allow the agent to take on responsibilities as soon as the papers are signed, or the agent may have privileges added or revoked at a certain time. It all depends on the language in the POA.

Normally, the POA is abdicated if the principal becomes incapacitated; however, if the principal chooses to put a durable POA into effect, the agent will be able to act on behalf of the principal even after incapacitation.

The following sections detail the different levels of power you can choose to give to your agent.

General Power of Attorney

This document is used when you want to give authority to an attorney-in-fact over certain defined aspects of your business matters. Perhaps you want that person to manage all real estate transactions, insurance matters, or operations of a given business.

You may also decide whether the agent may assign duties to another person. The general POA makes clear your intent in this case.

The general POA takes effect immediately upon signing. This document becomes invalid if you are rendered disabled or incapacitated.

Limited Power of Attorney

A limited POA makes sense when you need someone to act in your stead for a limited time only, or for just one purpose. This document specifies the precise areas of oversight, allowable decisions and actions, and often the period of time in which the agent will represent you.

The limited POA is appropriate for completing a certain transaction that must take place without your physical presence. Through a limited POA, you might designate an attorney-in-fact to handle transactions relating to a particular portion of your business, or you might complete the form to provide for financial management for a limited period of time. There are many instances in which naming your representative for a period of time or only for certain aspects of your affairs can be useful.

This document is annulled in the event of your incapacity, incompetence, or death. It is also annulled if you divorce.

Special versions of the limited POA form are available for real estate transactions and for the purposes of childcare.

Unlimited Power of Attorney

An unlimited POA gives the attorney-in-fact authority over any and all of your financial transactions and contracts. This particular form is the most detailed of all POA forms, providing thorough instructions regarding the actions an agent is allowed to take. Principals who want to limit the attorney-in-fact's powers need to use either a general or limited POA.

The unlimited POA specifically allows the attorney-in-fact to delegate duties to another person. Again, if this is not your intention, use the general POA.

The unlimited POA is automatically rendered invalid if you become incapacitated or incompetent. It is also annulled if you divorce or if you revoke the POA.

Limited POA for real estate

The POA for real estate allows an attorney-in-fact to buy or sell one specified piece of property. This form allows the real estate deal to go through via an agent, but does not allow the agent to represent you in other financial matters. Therefore, you can protect other financial assets, but still have the freedom to let your agent handle this transaction.

In many states, an official statutory form must be used when establishing a limited POA for real estate. But in other states, you will use the forms and processes required by the lender or title insurance company. The company you are working with will likely provide you with the form they prefer you to use.

The rules involved in executing a real estate POA are the same as the rules used in the signing of deeds in the state in which the property is located.

CASE STUDY: USING A POA IN BUSINESS AND FOR TAXES

Chuck McCollum
Los Angeles

I used a power of attorney about 12 years ago, when it was going to be helpful to have our business manager pay certain bills for my wife and me. Our finances were complicated, and our business manager was in place to negotiate better deals on areas like insurance, and auto and home purchases.

The first time I used a POA, it made me nervous. Although I trusted our business manager, there was still that sense of being vulnerable to having all our money ripped off. In the end, we did not encounter any trouble with the POA.

I also used a limited POA so my tax accountant could sign certain documents on my behalf when I was dealing with issues involving some unpaid back taxes. In the second case, I was not as nervous about the transaction because it was limited to tax-related documents with state and federal governments. In this case, there would have been nothing for my accountant to gain.

Durable Unlimited Power of Attorney

Finally, two types of durable unlimited POA are used to provide for oversight and management of your financial affairs. The first type of durable unlimited POA continues to be in effect throughout your life, even if you become disabled or incapacitated. However, it does expire upon your death.

The second type of durable unlimited POA becomes effective if you become incapacitated. This kind of POA is also called a *springing POA*, as it "springs" into effect if you become mentally or physically incapable.

Who will determine whether you are physically or mentally capable? Every state legislature provides guidelines for making such a determination and, commonly, the law tends to err on the side of the patient's rights and self-determination. Your health care POA will specify standards for making any judgments of incapacity, including certification by one or two physicians.

A durable unlimited POA grants unlimited powers in regard to financial affairs. If you wish to grant only a portion of the responsibility to another, you will need to use a limited POA.

None of the financial POAs pertain in any way to making decisions about your health. Your agent is responsible for money matters only, yet, the agent may need to examine and pay medical bills, so this POA form provides a release authorizing your agent to have access to these records.

Your attorney-in-fact is given the responsibility to make decisions and actions that are in your best interest. It is up to you to ensure your designee is well-informed regarding your preferences and to discuss matters with that person until you are relatively confident he or she understands your wishes.

Selecting a Financial Attorney-in-Fact

Carefully select your attorney-in-fact for financial matters. The choice of agent and his or her necessary skills will vary depending on whether the document is limited or unlimited, durable or general.

For example, an agent does not need wide-ranging management skills or to be a whiz at finances if you are merely establishing a limited POA to give the agent authority to transact all details related to the sale of a vacation home. You do, however, need to be able to trust this person to faithfully execute the assignment, making choices that are in your best interest.

On the other hand, you would want an agent with adequate management skills and financial know-how when establishing an unlimited POA, which gives the agent broad authority over your finances. You will also need to spend sufficient time with that person to familiarize this person on your business preferences in order to represent you properly. The following list gives state-specific information regarding powers given to agents who sign statutory POAs. Remember, most states have adopted statutory POAs to be used.

The statutory forms from the following states allow agents to have only the powers specifically stated in the POA document:

- Arkansas
- California
- Colorado
- District of Columbia
- Minnesota
- Montana
- Wisconsin
- North Carolina
- New York
- New Mexico
- Nebraska

The following states automatically give agents any and all powers unless the principal indicates otherwise on the POA form:

- Alaska
- Connecticut
- Texas
- Illinois

The following states only provide statutory forms for durable POAs:

- Florida
- Louisiana
- Missouri
- New Hampshire
- Virginia
- Pennsylvania
- Oregon
- Ohio

To create other types of POAs in these states, respectively, you will need to create your own POA documents or forms, recommended by legal counsel from your state.

To Review:

A financial POA allows your agent or surrogate to represent you in financial matters. These may include the purchase of items, property, investments, or other banking transactions.

You may choose to give your agent:

- Limited POAs if you want to restrict your agent to a particular type or number of transactions

- Unlimited POAs if you want your agent to be able to handle any transaction on your behalf

- Limited real estate POA if you want your agent to be able to handle the purchase or sale of a piece of property, but do not want him or her to have access to your other financial business

Normally, the POA is abdicated if you become incapacitated; however, if you choose to put a durable POA into effect, your agent will still be able to act on your behalf even after your incapacitation.

CASE STUDY: USING A POA FOR HEALTH CARE

Casey Burke,
New York

I am a social worker working with people who have mental illnesses or are living with HIV/AIDS. Many of the people I work with have given power of attorney over to someone else, such as a family member, friend, or case management organization. They do not feel that they can make financial decisions for themselves any longer due to the symptoms and incapacitation brought on by their illnesses.

Certain types of POA can only be enacted after consulting with the person whose affairs are being taken over. However, most of the people I work with who require a POA have given durable power of attorney to a family member or friend. In such cases, the agent does not have to consult the principal regarding the latter's affairs. At times, this can lead to patients losing their independence before it is warranted, simply because they had the foresight to put a POA into action. When the person they have appointed does not respect their wishes, money may be spent in a manner of which the principal does not approve. This can lead to the principal being neglected or not cared for appropriately because the agent may not have the principal's best interests at heart and may be misusing the funds and the power entrusted.

In order to avoid problems with POAs, people should put their explicit wishes in writing as to the way they would like their money spent and the types of care for which they are willing to pay. In many cases, this is where neglect happens. And of the utmost importance is choosing someone you can trust to respect your wishes and to understand the value of maintaining the highest quality of life possible for as long as is possible.

Chapter 6

Medical and Health Care POA

MEET THE JONESES

George Jones makes a preliminary trip to meet his friend Alan at the vacation home site and go over the setup of things. They also exchange fully executed copies of their POA documents. When they take a break for some supper at the nearby seafood joint, George mentions his concern about Diane's health.

"It is nothing really obvious," George says. "It is just… I am noticing how we are not getting any younger."

His friend laughs. But then he gets serious and starts talking about how he has been thinking about the same things: getting old, becoming sick, or maybe losing your memory and even forgetting who you are.

"I have signed advance directives to make sure I do not totally lose all control when the doctors are treating me," Alan tells George.

On the plane flying home, George mulls over his friend's words and wonders how Diane would prefer to be treated if she were incapable of making her own decisions. For that matter, what would be his own preferences if he were too sick or too old to think?

George's daughter, Kristin, is way ahead of him. Through her contact with the medical field, she is aware of medical and health care powers of attorney. A savvy planner, Kristin has already obtained a durable POA for health care in which she intends to name her father as attorney-in-fact to prepare for any accidents that could befall her when she travels.

When George arrives home from his trip, Kristin calls to tell him about this and arranges to get together with the following weekend for a serious chat. George marvels at his daughter's prescience: Did she know this very issue was also on his mind?

In recent years, technological advances in medicine and health have resulted in people living much longer than previously. When we are ill, near death, or injured in an accident, technology often allows us to prolong life extensively.

But concerns about personal privacy and individual rights mean that choice-making is an extremely delicate matter in the health industry. The controversies surrounding such famous end-of-life cases as those of Karen Ann Quinlan, Nancy Cruzan, and Theresa Schiavo have brought to light the difficult tension between the individual's right-to-die and the medical imperative to preserve life at all costs.

Health care issues can become intensely personal and heated. Having a POA that spells out your health care wishes can save loved ones time and money, as well as reduce stress and protect the state of their relationships.

Noteworthy Right-to-Die Cases

Karen Ann Quinlan

Karen Ann Quinlan was born in 1954. When she was 21, she moved in with friends and reportedly went on a serious diet to lose weight. She weighed 115 pounds shortly before entering into the annals of the right-to-die debate.

Quinlan went to a party after allegedly eating practically nothing for two days. At a bar, she reportedly had a couple of cocktails and swallowed a tranquilizer. Shortly thereafter, she felt faint and friends took her home to bed. Approximately 15 minutes later, friends reported that they found her in bed, not breathing. They began CPR and called for an ambulance. Quinlan did not regain consciousness.

She was taken to the hospital and remained in a coma. Doctors said that Quinlan suffered irreversible brain damage and was in a persistent vegetative state. This means a patient exhibits some basic reflexes, but no significant cognitive function — they do not exhibit the ability to make decisions, think, or mentally respond to stimulus. Her eyes no longer moved in the same direction, and an EEG showed minimal brain activity.

Quinlan remained in a coma, and in the hospital, for several months. She suffered seizures and had to be put on feeding and breathing tubes. Many thought these tubes were the only thing keeping her alive.

After months of seeing their loved one in this state, Quinlan's family requested that she be taken off the machines and allowed to die. But doctors and hospital staff refused to comply with their request.

Eventually the family took their case to the New Jersey Supreme Court. The court ruled in the family's favor and stated that doctors must take Quinlan off the ventilator.

To the surprise of many, however, Quinlan continued to breathe and lived on a feeding tube for nine more years. She did not, however, regain consciousness and finally died of pneumonia in 1985.

This was the first case to deal with the issue of continuing or ending treatment that prolongs a person's life when it is in doubt whether the patient would survive without the treatment. Previously, the courts had not ruled on a where a person could not speak on their own behalf and make decisions about such drastic treatment.

Nancy Cruzan

Another important story in the right to life debate is the case of Nancy Cruzan. Cruzan was born in 1957, and in 1983 she was in a terrible car accident. Her car flipped off the road, landed in a ditch, and left the 25-year-old Cruzan unconscious.

Cruzan was found approximately 15 minutes after her accident. She was facedown in the ditch, and paramedics could not detect breathing or a heartbeat. They were, however, able to revive her, and her heartbeat and breathing returned. But Cruzan did not regain consciousness.

She was taken to a hospital, where doctors stated she had significant contusions on her brain. Courts and medical professionals had previously determined that permanent brain damage can occur after a person has not been breathing for six minutes. Cruzan, officials predicted, had stopped breathing for 12 to 14 minutes before paramedics found her by the side of the road. It seemed unlikely that she would be able to escape serious brain damage.

In the hospital, Cruzan remained in a coma. In the coma, Cruzan was still able to take food through her mouth. After approximately three weeks, she slipped into complete unconsciousness. Her husband allowed hospital staff to put a feeding tube and a hydration tube in Cruzan. Doctors continued to try to revive her, but those attempts were unsuccessful.

Cruzan was in a persistent vegetative state, and after four years of no progress, Cruzan's family finally decided it would be best to remove the tubes and let her die. The hospital, however, would not comply with their wishes. The family went to court locally, but the state of Missouri would not allow the family to take out the tubes. The case was brought before the Supreme Court. It took three years of litigation to come to a conclusion. In 1990, the courts let Cruzan's family remove the tube. She died 11 days after the removal.

Terri Schiavo

In February of 1990, Schiavo collapsed in her Florida home. Her husband, Michael, called 911; paramedics arrived to find her unconscious, not breathing, and without a pulse. Many attempts were made to revive her, and she was taken to the hospital. There, a breathing tube was inserted into her lungs, and she was eventually given a tracheotomy.

Doctors believed her collapse was due to a lack of nourishment. Her brain was without oxygen for an extended period of time between her collapse and the arrival of paramedics. It is likely that severe brain damage had set in by this time.

After two months in a coma, Schiavo seemed to be making progress. She started showing a sleep cycle, but she did not show a consistent pattern of being aware of herself or her environment. She also still could not feed herself, so doctors inserted a feeding tube directly into her stomach through her abdominal wall.

Approximately a year after her collapse, doctors from two institutions made the diagnosis that Schiavo was in a persistent vegetative state.

Her family decided to bring her home from the hospital and care for her themselves. However, they soon found this impossible, so Schiavo was brought back to the hospital. They continued to try drastic measures to revive her. Michael even took his wife to the University of California, San Francisco, for an experimental procedure involving an electrical stimulator placed in Schiavo's brain. Michael brought Schiavo back home to Florida, where more attempts were made to bring Schiavo back to cognitive awareness. She was taken on walks and outings, and therapists and doctors worked with her.

In 1993, three years after her collapse, Schiavo contracted a urinary tract infection. Michael decided to set up a do not resuscitate (DNR) order on behalf of his wife. After conversations with doctors and three years of trying to save her life, Michael seemed to feel his wife's life was essentially over.

But while Michael wanted to remove the life support machines, the Schindlers — Schiavo's relatives — did not want that to happen. The two parties went back and forth with court proceedings regarding the removal of life support machines.

Michael petitioned the courts to act as Schiavo's surrogate (or agent). Eventually, Michael relinquished control to the courts as the family debated what do to. Michael said that Schiavo had previously stated she did not want extreme measures to be taken to prolong her life if the issue ever came up. But with no documentation in place, there was no way to prove for certain what Schiavo would have wanted.

In 1998, Michael petitioned to have Schiavo's feeding tube removed. The family countered. They did not want their daughter to die by dehydration — the cause of death of many people in a persistent vegetative state after their feeding tube is removed.

The Schindler family and the courts felt pressure to protect Schiavo's wishes and her resources. However, there was also the possibly of Schiavo's family inheriting her estate. Because of these complications, and the fact that Schiavo did not have a living will, court officials said that she must remain on life support.

In 2000, a trial was held to determine what Schiavo would have wanted, were she able to speak for herself in this situation. Michael insisted his wife would not want to be kept on life support machines if there was no hope for her recovery. But the Schindlers said Schiavo was a strict Catholic who would have thought removing life support would violate her religious beliefs. The judge for the case gave Michael the right to discontinue the procedures that were keeping his wife alive. But the family responded with further court appeals. Later in 2000, they petitioned the court to allow them to feed Schiavo without the use of the tubes. Doctors said feeding Schiavo without the assistance of tubes would not be possible, as she would be unable to swallow, so the family's request was denied.

In another appeal, the Schindler family alleged that Michael did not provide the proper care and attention Schiavo needed while she was in the hospital because Michael has pursued a relationship with another woman. They used this accusation to challenge his guardianship in the hope of having it revoked. Michael stated that he chose to stay legally married to Schiavo to protect his wishes through his position as guardian. Had he divorced her while she was in a persistent vegetative state, guardianship would have transferred to her family. A judge did not find sufficient evidence to remove Michael's guardianship.

Schiavo's feeding tube was removed in April 2001, and the Schindlers filed a perjury suit against Michael. A judge ordered the tube was to be reinserted until the case was finalized. Ultimately, the tube stayed in place.

The family changed their tactics at that point. Instead of insisting that Michael was an unfit legal guardian, they alleged that Schiavo was not in a persistent vegetative state. They asserted she was in a "minimally conscious state." They said Schiavo laughed, smiled, moved, tried to speak, and showed other signs of consciousness. Some medical evidence suggested otherwise, however.

The Schindlers went back to court in the fall of 2001, but were unsuccessful in their attempts to get their daughter's state of being reclassified.

The courts looked at evidence again to determine whether newer treatments could possibly help Schiavo regain consciousness. Doctors reviewed hours of footage and heard testimonies from several doctors. The judge in the case ruled that Schiavo was in a persistent vegetative state, and her condition was beyond the scope of what doctors could do to help her regain consciousness.

The Schindlers produced a short video featuring hopeful moments of a day in the life of Terri Schiavo. They posted this video on the Internet and began to gain national attention for their daughter's state. The six minutes of the video were not consecutive, however, and were cobbled together from a time period of six hours; the bulk of which, a judge said, showed that Schiavo was likely beyond hope.

In October 2003, Schiavo's tube was removed, but the family worked swiftly to change that. The Florida government passed what became known as "Terri's Law." This law allowed former Florida Governor Jeb Bush to intervene in the situation. He ordered that her feeding tube be reinserted. Michael, with support from the American Civil Liberties Union (ACLU), challenged Terri's Law. The Florida Supreme Court eventually overturned the law, citing that it was unconstitutional.

In March 2005, doctors removed Schiavo's feeding tube for the third time. The case became intensely political, eventually involving the U.S. Congress. The matter was ultimately turned over to the Federal Supreme Court, who declined to review the case.

Schiavo died on March 31, 2005. She had been in a vegetative state for 15 years when she died.

The Aftermath

The controversies that surrounded the previous right-to-die cases in the late 20th century led to a new understanding of the need for durable health care POAs. Before these cases, few people knew about advance directives or about appointing a health care surrogate. The affects — both emotional and physical — of not having a document outlining a potential patient's wishes or indicating who is to make the decisions on behalf the patient is clear from these well-known cases. In the case of Terri Schiavo, relationships were torn and tortured. And in all three cases, costly medical care continued, possibly leading to devastatingly high medical bills. A clear set of directions and someone to carry out those directions could have helped avoid that trouble. Consequently, today, attending to these documents is a relatively well-known practice.

Not all medical choice-making is life-or-death; there are many treatment options in most health situations. Normally, the physician is expected to carefully explain these options and allow the patient to choose one. Because making such decisions is often not be possible when you are unwell, it makes sense to officially appoint another individual to represent your interests during medical treatments. That is the point of a medical power of attorney.

The attorney-in-fact can ensure your interests and preferences are expressed to attending medical personnel. The health care agent should also have a copy of your living will.

Impact of the Quinlan, Cruzan, and Schiavo Cases

The cases of Quinlan, Cruzan, and Schiavo were all milestones in the right-to-die debate. These three women became incapacitated in very different circumstances, and the dilemmas presented by their conditions were not exactly alike. But they all raised one profoundly difficult question: If a person is persistently unresponsive as a result of some kind of trauma or illness, who has the authority to make choices for them?

A century ago, this would not have been a pressing issue simply because we did not have the technology to prolong life that we have today; each of the previously mentioned women probably would have been left for dead a century ago. Cruzan had been lying facedown in a ditch, not breathing for many minutes before medics managed to revive her. Quinlan was found unconscious in bed. Schiavo was also unconscious when paramedics found her.

As technology has advanced, new questions are being asked and need to be answered. The rights of the individual are at the core of the issue. When someone is in such dire straits — to the point that life is only sustained by machines and tools such as breathing and feeding tubes — what should be done? Who gets to decide which treatments are performed and whether all measures have been exhausted?

The traditional legal definition of "dead" meant a person's cardiac and respiratory systems stopped working and could not be made to work again; that is to say that CPR or other methods such as defibrillation do not cause the heart and lungs to begin working again. But the advent of technology now allows doctors to see brain function, thus states now consider the Uniform Determination of Death Act (UDDA) when determining whether a person is dead. This act, adopted in 1981, says a person can be considered dead when one of two things is apparent: Either the heart and lungs have stopped working on their own and cannot be started again, or brain function has stopped and cannot be started again.

However, a person who is "brain dead" — that is, they do not show brain function — may still exhibit signs of being alive. Their bodies may be warm, and rigor mortis will not set in. Bodies of people who are brain dead may also continue some functions including digestion and excretion. Their bodies may even continue to grow. Despite these outward expressions of what many would call "life," a brain dead person can be considered legally dead, according to the UDDA. The science of brain death, however, does not make it any easier for family members to let go of a loved one, and thus the stage is set for stories like the ones you read about earlier in this chapter.

Religion, faith, and philosophical beliefs can also play a part in family members' decisions regarding their loved ones' right to remain on — or be taken off — life support. Euthanasia is when a person enlists the help of someone else to end his or her life. Usually this happens when someone is terminally ill, very sick, or in a lot of pain.

In the 1990s, Dr. Jack Kevorkian helped bring euthanasia into the spotlight when he was an outspoken proponent of patients being allowed to decide if they should die. He assisted at least 130 people in ending their lives. For this, Kevorkian served eight years in prison on second-degree murder charges.

Some agreed with Kevorkian. Many people felt that if a person wanted to end their life, they had a right to do so with dignity, and help if they needed it. However, courts made it clear that doctor-supported euthanasia is illegal.

On the other hand, some see removing life support as a form of euthanasia. Because of this, many people have an understandably difficult time with the concept. Legally, courts have ruled that removing life support is not the same as euthanasia. Thanks to statues like the UDDA, hospitals and other medical care facilities are relieved of this emotional decision and are allowed to make decisions about whether a patient is alive or dead based on measurable scientific evidence. But as was seen in the Schiavo case, some doctors may find nuance in a patient's condition that may make it more difficult for laypeople to understand their prognoses.

Having a POA in place may not make dealing with a sick or injured family member any easier, but it can remove the burden of the decision from loved ones. It also allows the patient to have the end of life — or the continuation of life — that he or she prefers.

The cases presented earlier in this chapter were complicated by the fact that the three women had not prepared health care POAs, and the courts were charged with sorting out the personal preferences of the principals. The judgments handed down by the courts after considering the legalities of these landmark cases have eventually resulted in federal mandates regarding living wills and language about advance directives, including durable health care POAs, in the statutes of every state in the United States.

Durable Health Care or Medical POA

A medical emergency can happen at any time. Perhaps you are in an auto accident and are unconscious for a brief period. Maybe you become incapacitated after a dangerous but accidental combination of alcohol and medication. A durable health care or medical POA names a representative for health-related matters in the event of your incapacity. Having a designated advocate in your attorney-in-fact can ensure that your interests and preferences are well-conveyed to your attending medical personnel.

Unlike nondurable financial POAs, the durable health care POA remains in effect or is activated if you become incapacitated, and it does not change if you get divorced.

The durable health care POA does not confer authority over any financial matters. It also is only a portion of the complete preparation for end-of-life care. If you are completing a durable health care POA to become effective upon your disability or incapacity, you will also need to complete a living will and other advance health care directives. *See Chapter 7 for more information on these auxiliary documents.*

Choosing an Attorney-in-Fact for Health Care

When selecting the attorney-in-fact for a durable health care POA, it is important to consider the emotional strength and confidence of the person. If your spouse is likely to be too distraught to make decisions if you become incapacitated, name a trusted friend or other relative instead.

Your agent should be willing and able to interact effectively with medical personnel. This person does not need to have a medical background, but must be able to aggressively pursue your interests in a medical situation.

It is impossible to anticipate all possible medical situations, but it is crucial to have a serious discussion with your attorney-in-fact *in advance*. Express your feelings about various procedures with the agent. Consider such admittedly difficult questions as:

- Your wishes about prolonging life if you are in a vegetative state

- Medical treatments you would sanction or reject

- Whether or not you would choose to have water and nutrition withdrawn or other forms of life support removed if you are mentally incapacitated and near death

Discuss these preferences with your attorney-in-fact. Do not sign the POA unless you are confident the agent understands your wishes and can be trusted to act accordingly.

Having this discussion with your attorney-in-fact is extremely important, and because it is a difficult conversation, sometimes people name agents without going over the specifics with the individual in question. But though you may implicitly trust that person, unless you clearly verbalize your wishes, you cannot assume he or she will accurately intuit them.

Living Wills

Your health care agent should also have a copy of your living will. The power of attorney document should be enough to allow your agent to make decisions on your behalf. However, if questions, issues, or objections are raised — by family members, for example, who object to the decisions your agent is making — the living will can be produced as evidence of your wishes.

A living will outlines the types of medical treatment or procedures you would accept in the event that you are unable to speak for yourself at the time those procedures need to be performed. Generally, a living will only addresses procedures considered extreme or "life-prolonging," such as CPR, feeding, or breathing tubes.

The law generally allows living wills to be applied in any of these three situations:

- **A patient in a persistent vegetative state**. Patients in this state are unable to make decisions on their own. The fact that responses sometimes may be detected in these patients is enough to give family and friends hope. Without a living will that expresses the patient's wishes, it is more difficult to know whether to remove life-prolonging machines.

- **A patient in an end-stage condition**. An end-stage condition is one in which a doctor or medical professional has determined that a patient is in such a severe condition that recovery is unlikely to a reasonable medical certainty. This condition could be the result of a large-scale accident or a debilitating disease.

- **A patient in a terminal condition**. A terminal condition occurs when a person is suffering with a disease or injury that cannot be cured. People who have a terminal condition would die without medical treatment as the disease or injury runs its course.

See Chapter 7 for more information on living wills.

What is Right for You?

Just because you have determined that some sort of advance directive is best for you does not mean you are clear as to what you want that advance directive to say. You may know you want to give someone attorney-in-fact powers regarding your medical needs should you become incapacitated, but you may not know what you want them to do on your behalf. The following sections offer descriptions of important terms and concepts you should be familiar with when preparing your health care POA.

Important terms and concepts to know

Persistent vegetative state versus coma

Your brain behaves differently depending on the state of unconsciousness and where the injury to your brain is. It is important to understand these differences so you can make an educated decision about medical treatment that you would prefer to have rendered should you end up unconscious and unable to speak for yourself.

A persistent vegetative state (PVS) occurs when a person's brain has been deprived of oxygen in the areas that control thinking, feeling, and communication. The person is unconscious and cannot respond except by unconscious reflex. A person in a PVS can likely breathe on his or her own. The body may exhibit the properties of waking and sleeping, but the person in a PVS displays no indication of the ability to see or hear, regardless of whether or not his or her eyes are open or closed.

Most PVS patients are unresponsive to external stimuli, and their conditions are associated with different levels of consciousness. Some level of consciousness means a person can still respond, in varying degrees, to stimulation. A person in a coma, however, cannot. In addition, PVS patients often open their eyes in response to feeding, which has to be done by others; they are capable of swallowing, whereas patients in a coma subsist with their eyes closed.

PVS patients' eyes might be in a relatively fixed position, or track moving objects, or even move in an unsynchronized manner. They may exhibit some behaviors that can be construed as arising from partial consciousness, such as grinding their teeth, swallowing, smiling, shedding tears, grunting, moaning, or screaming without any apparent external stimulus.

Individuals in PVS are seldom on any life-sustaining equipment other than a feeding tube because the brainstem — the center of vegetative functions such as heart rate and rhythm, respiration, and gastrointestinal activity — is relatively intact.

A coma is another way of describing the state of a person when he or she is unconscious. Someone in a coma cannot respond to stimulation. There are two types of comas: reversible and irreversible. A reversible coma usually occurs after a quick trauma, such as a drug overdose or sudden accident. It is medically more likely than not that a person in a reversible coma eventually will regain consciousness.

An irreversible coma occurs when there is massive trauma to the brain that cannot be repaired after the brain has been deprived of oxygen. In these types of comas, a person is continuously in a sleeplike state and does not display periods that resemble wakefulness.

The severity of coma impairment is categorized into several levels. Patients may or may not progress through these levels. In the first level, the brain responsiveness lessens, normal reflexes are lost, and the patient no longer responds to pain and cannot hear.

Outcomes range from recovery to death. Comas generally last a few days to a few weeks. They rarely last more than 2 to 5 weeks, but some have lasted as long as several years. After this time, some patients gradually come out of the coma, some progress to a vegetative state, and some others die. Some patients who have entered a vegetative state go on to regain a degree of awareness. Others remain in a vegetative state for years or even decades.

The outcome for a coma and vegetative state depends on the cause, location, severity, and extent of neurological damage. A deeper coma alone does not necessarily mean a slimmer chance of recovery, because some people in deep coma recover well, while others in a so-called milder coma sometimes fail to improve.

People may emerge from a coma with a combination of physical, intellectual, and psychological difficulties that need special attention. Recovery usually occurs gradually — patients acquire more and more ability to respond. Some patients never progress beyond very basic responses, but many recover full awareness. Regaining consciousness is not instant: In the first days, patients are only awake for a few minutes, and duration of time awake gradually increases.

Life-sustaining therapies

It is reported that five to ten percent of all coma patients persist in a vegetative, nonresponsive, long-term comatose state. While it is unlikely that a person will regain consciousness after a long coma, it is not impossible, and there are several techniques medical professionals use to give patients the best chance of recovery. In general, these techniques are referred to as "life-sustaining therapies." It is important to understand what these therapies involve so you can make specific and educated decisions about your medical care.

Artificial feeding

Whether you are able to feed yourself or not, your body needs food to survive. Medical professionals have many ways of helping comatose patients receive the nutrients they need. Some incapacitated patients reflexively respond to stimulus, so medical professionals are able to feed them orally with solid food or a liquid blend of food. Some patients, however, do not exhibit the reflexes and muscle movement involved in eating, so these patients require a tube to be inserted into their stomachs and intravenous lines that allow nutrients to pass directly into the blood stream. These patients may require hydration to be delivered intravenously as well.

This artificial feeding keeps the person from dying of starvation or dehydration. Without a significant change in the patient's condition, the patient will die if the artificial means of feeding are stopped.

People may disagree about whether artificial feeding methods are basic medical provisions that doctors should provide, or whether artificial feeding prolongs a patient's life unnecessarily. Likewise, some people feel that stopping artificial feeding is in direct conflict with a doctor's ethical oath. Others may feel that stopping artificial feeding is simply allowing the body to do what it wants, what is natural. Death by starvation or dehydration can be extremely painful for a person in a normal, waking state. For this reason, many may object to inflicting a possibly painful method of death on a loved one. Others may question whether a person in a coma or persistent vegetative state can have a conscious feeling of the pain a waking person would.

Doctors often give patients pain relievers when they remove feeding apparatuses. They also help patients with other comfort issues — they continue to clean the patients and keep their mouths and eyes moist. Also, any other medicine the patient is on will still be given. These steps help ensure that a dying patient — even a comatose one — remains comfortable and feels as little pain as possible.

Ventilators

A ventilator is a machine that mechanically moves air in and out of a patient's lungs when the patient is unable to breathe naturally without assistance. Ventilators do this through an air reservoir and a series of tubes and valves. The machine pushes air into the patient's lungs. When the set amount of air has been pushed into the lungs, the pressure from the machine is released. When the pressure is released, the patient's lungs will naturally compress, pushing the air back out of the lungs. This process is repeated continuously in a breathing rhythm.

If a person cannot breathe on his or her own, clearly the condition and upkeep of the ventilator is extremely important. Ventilators are often equipped with backup power sources so the machine can keep working in case of a power outage. A ventilator is considered a "life-critical system" because of how important it is to a patient's ability to sustain life.

Modern ventilators, which involve tubes inserted into a patient's mouth or nose, had their start with less invasive — but much more cumbersome — equipment, like the iron lung. The iron lung was developed in the early part of the 20th century. Patients would lie inside the iron lung like a caterpillar in a cocoon with only their head sticking out of these giant machines. The iron lungs used negative air pressure to cause the patients' lungs to expand and contract, which enabled the patients' bodies to breathe. Unfortunately, patients inside iron lungs were confined to a life of lying on their backs so the machine could breathe for them.

While medical ventilators provide a vital and necessary part of treatment for patients, the devices do not come without risks. Artificially inflating the lungs can cause tearing. When the brain is shut down and a machine is taking breaths for the patient, the pain mechanism cannot stop the lungs from expanding if the machine should put too much air into the lungs. Sometimes if a patient recovers, their lungs will be so scarred from tearing that they will always require constant treatment.

Patients on ventilators are more likely to get a form of pneumonia called "ventilator-assisted pneumonia." Each year, more than 200,000 patients on ventilators are diagnosed with this condition. Approximately 15 percent of hospital deaths are caused by pneumonia. The bacteria that cause pneumonia can easily grow in the tubing inserted into patients. And while pneumonia is treatable, it can be difficult to diagnose. Especially in unconscious patients who cannot express pain or discomfort.

Despite these risks, medical professionals have found ways of combating some of these issues. Certain chemicals applied to the tubes to the patient's mucous membranes can help slow the rate of infection and lower the overall risk of infection to a patient.

Basic CPR and defibrillation

CPR stands for cardiopulmonary resuscitation. It is a life-saving technique that can be used after a heart attack, when a person has almost drowned, or any other time when a person's heart has stopped or they have stopped breathing.

When a person delivers CPR, he or she uses chest compressions to mimic the heart's natural beat, and they breathe into the person's mouth to mimic the natural breath that a person draws into the lungs outside of a traumatic event.

CPR is a relatively easy life-saving method to learn, and communities often offer many ways to learn how to deliver CPR. Because it will take emergency personnel at least a few minutes to arrive at an accident or trauma scene, CPR can keep an accident victim alive before an ambulance or emergency team is available. A few extra heartbeats or breaths of oxygen can be the difference between life, severe brain trauma, or death.

If a person's heart stops, and oxygen-rich blood is no longer being circulated around the body, severe and permanent brain damage can happen in just a few minutes. The person can die within 10 minutes of a person's heart stopping. Providing CPR can give an accident victim a realistic chance of recovery.

Defibrillation is another type of treatment given when a person's heart stops beating. Historically, this procedure has been performed by medical professionals. Doctors or other hospital or emergency staff use two paddles to deliver an electric shock to the chest. The shock is intended to jump-start the patient's heart back into a normal rhythm.

Recently, however, home and office defibrillators have become available so that laypeople can work to save the lives of loved ones. Some of these machines consist of the typical hand-held paddles, while others consist of two flaps of material filled with electric conductors. Regardless of the construction of the machine, it is connected to an electricity source that carries enough charge to deliver up to a few shocks. These machines can often help buy time while rescue workers and medical professionals arrive.

There are other ways to deliver defibrillation, including applying conductors directly to the heart muscle. This type of defibrillation is typically done when a person is undergoing open-heart surgery and goes into cardiac arrest.

Every life-saving technique comes with its benefits and risks. As a potential patient, you must consider these risks and rewards and determine what would be best for you.

CASE STUDY: A NURSE'S VIEW OF POAS

Nathan Jones
Registered Nurse

When patients are initially placed on a ventilator, it is usually in the setting of an emergency; a patient must be intubated (have an endotracheal tube inserted via nose or mouth) to be placed on a ventilator. A conscious patient must be sedated and then paralyzed with medication in order to pass the endotracheal tube. In an unconscious patient, medication may not be necessary.

Once the patient is intubated, correct placement of the tube is confirmed (via listening for equal bilateral breath sounds, checking for color change on a commercially-available end-tidal CO2 detector, and visualizing the tube on a chest x-ray). The patient is then connected from the endotracheal tube to the tubing of the ventilator itself. In the otherwise conscious patient, the patient must be kept on sedating medication in order to tolerate the ventilator. In patients with severe brain injury, medication may not be necessary.

A gastric feeding tube can be placed directly into the stomach. This is done in the operating room. Short-term feeding tubes can be inserted at the bedside, and these tubes are inserted via the nose. Placement then is confirmed by X-ray.

CPR is performed on the patient with a non-perfusing cardiac arrhythmia. CPR guidelines are dictated by the American Heart Association. In the hospital setting, one provider is responsible for chest compressions, while another provides breaths with a bag-valve-mask (typically called an "ambu bag"). In the field, if there is only one provider, the provider will alternate chest compressions and breath delivery according to the guidelines.

Defibrillation is performed only on patients with specific non-perfusing arrhythmias, which are indicated in ACLS (advanced cardiac life support) guidelines published by the American Heart Association.

Risks with the above procedures include incorrect tube placement (with intubation and feeding tubes), which, if uncorrected, can lead to hypoxia and aspiration. Intubation should not be painful if the patient is adequately sedated and paralyzed. Insertion of the feeding tube is uncomfortable, for sure, because of a patient's gag reflex. Defibrillation is painful (it can cause burns) if the paddles are not adequately coated with conducting gel; however, if someone requires defibrillation, they are not conscious to feel it.

Patients can have normal life expectancy, even if they are ventilator-dependent and require a feeding tube for their nutrition.

Patients on the vent have higher risk of pneumonia because they cannot clear their own secretions (cough) to remove phlegm the way a non-intubated person can; oral hygiene is decreased, and build-up of oral bacteria can cause infection. Also, a patient can aspirate stomach contents into the lungs, causing an aspiration-pneumonia.

Beneficial treatment versus nonbeneficial treatment

Depending on the severity of the illness or accident, doctors may determine that some treatments are beneficial and some treatments are nonbeneficial. Beneficial treatments are those that are likely to produce a positive effect. They are treatments that will most likely lead to a patient's recovery. The term may also be applied when a patient's condition is not so severe that doctors believe there is little chance for survival.

Nonbeneficial treatment is just the opposite. Nonbeneficial treatment is likely to produce no discernable effect on a patient, other than keeping the body alive. If a patient is unlikely to be able to recover even with certain treatments, those treatments are said to be nonbeneficial.

A doctor can give his or her opinion as to whether a treatment is beneficial or not. Some doctors may not want to perform treatment that they feel is nonbeneficial, so it is possible that they may not mention a treatment if they do not think it will be beneficial.

If you are healthy, you may want to ask your doctor to tell you about the wide range of life-sustaining treatments that are available. If you are ill, and the prognosis is grim, you can request that your doctor tell you about all the treatments available, whether he or she thinks they are beneficial or not, so that you can make a fully informed decision.

While there is an objective definition of beneficial and nonbeneficial treatment, you are allowed to have your own subjective definition of the same terms. You may think that remaining alive, even without recovering, is beneficial. If that is the case, request through your advance directive that any and all measures be taken to sustain your life.

You should know, however, that doctors are not required by law to give a patient treatments that they feel are nonbeneficial. They may refer you to some other physicians, but none of them will be obligated to provide a service that they think will not help.

CASE STUDY: Q&A ABOUT POWER OF ATTORNEY OPTIONS

Kim Downes
Registered Nurse

What type of power of attorney do you have experience with?
Medical

Why should someone consider having a power of attorney?
It will help let others know your wishes and save them a lot of hassles legally if you become incapacitated. It is a courtesy to those who may have to care for you or what you leave behind.

At what time in their lives should people prepare powers of attorney?
As an adult when they want their wishes made, or when they have accumulated anything of value.

What potential pitfalls are there to having someone to act on your behalf?
Medically, I've seen family wishes override the patient's wishes. People need to make it *very* clear what their wishes are to their families, have it spelled out, and express how they want them carried out. Also, if you no longer trust the person to act in your behalf, you have to go through the effort to change your power of attorney.

Should you have more than one person designated to act in your place?

That could lead to other problems. I think it is best to have *one* trusted person.

When is a "do not resuscitate" order appropriate? How can you best see that those wishes are followed?

Spell it out if you wish to be resuscitated at all costs, or if there is little to no risk of brain damage, or not at all. Anyone who has watched resuscitation on a futile situation knows how brutal it can be. It would be *very* wise to get medical opinions before making such a decision.

How did you/would you choose the individual to act in your place?

It needs to be someone you trust. That person is not always a family member. I had a friend who had medical power of attorney for her friend, as she did not trust her husband to make wise decisions on her behalf.

What potential pitfalls are there to agreeing to act on someone's behalf?

You may change your mind, have a falling out with that person, or have your own personal challenges that preclude you from fulfilling the person's wishes.

How to Make a Decision

No one but you can make the final decision about what you want to be done for you if you are badly injured or very sick. There is no right or wrong answer; there is only what makes you feel most comfortable. Weigh the risks and rewards of the various forms of care and life-sustaining treatments before deciding what will be best for you.

It may be comforting to know that most legal institutions do not consider refusing or stopping life-sustaining treatments to be suicide (from the patient's perspective) or murder or manslaughter (from the medical professional's perspective).

Stopping treatment once it has begun, or refusing life-sustaining treatment altogether, would not be the actual cause of the patient's death. In the courts' eyes, the disease or accident is the cause of death. This bit of information may also ease the minds of loved ones who would be concerned about legal ramifications if they were to stop treatment or refuse treatment on your behalf.

To make a decision about what life-sustaining measures you want performed on your behalf — if any — determine whether the benefits of that treatment outweigh the stress put on your body, and the emotions of your family and friends. If you were to recover, would life with severe limitations be worth living? Does it make financial sense to pay for an extended hospital stay and treatment if there is little hope of recovery?

Again, there are no right or wrong answers to these questions. These decisions are very personal and combine ideas of faith, philosophy, and finances. Because they are such personal and important decisions, you may wish to speak to a counselor, minister, or doctor to help you determine your values and priorities for these issues. Regardless of what discussion you have with any of these people, none of them have the right to contest your decision once you have made your wishes known and created your POA, living will, or any other form of advance directive.

Consult your physician

Talking with doctors about all the possibilities involved in end of life decisions will help you to make an educated decision about what you want to ultimately communicate to an attorney-in-fact. Doctors are not just there to treat medical problems once they arise; they are also available to help you decide how to manage medical problems before you actually have to face them. You may also want to speak with your doctors about conditions for which you are at risk. Depending on your state of health, activity level, family history, and even your job, you may be at a higher risk for certain illnesses or conditions.

To Review:

A health care POA allows someone to act on your behalf if you are unable to do so yourself. It is possible that you may fall ill or be in an accident where you are not able to speak for yourself. If that happens to you, you will need someone to speak on your behalf.

Before you assign your health care POA agent the duties they will be responsible for, you will need to determine what your wishes are if you find yourself injured or sick to the point where you cannot speak for yourself.

There are many reasons why you might find yourself unable to make your wishes known. A serious accident or a debilitating illness may result in a coma, general unconscious state, or persistent vegetative state. There is some help available in each of these conditions, but there are risks and variables to consider as well. The decision to accept life-sustaining treatment is a very personal decision and combines ideas of faith, philosophy, finances, and what type of burden you wish to put on your family. You may find it helpful to speak with medical professionals as well as people within your faith to help you determine what you wish to have happen to you if you become injured or sick.

Every treatment a hospital can offer a patient comes with risks and rewards. Nutritional therapies allow patients to continue being fed if they are not able to be fed orally. However, the tubes that are put into a person's body can be painful or uncomfortable. People can live very long lives on ventilators, but they also run a higher risk of catching pneumonia because the tubes can scratch the delicate mucous membranes in the body. Anything inserted in the body can also carry pathogens on it, no matter how clean the hospital or medical facility tries to keep it. And if a person is unconscious, he or she may not be able to convey pain or other symptoms of sickness. This can make resulting conditions more severe than they would be otherwise.

Chapter 7

Other Documents to Consider in Addition to Your POA

MEET THE JONESES

Fast-forward nine months in the lives of the Jones family. George and his friend Alan have made good progress on the vacation home, although commuting and spending so much free time on this second job are beginning to wear on George. He is making good money, but is glad it will be over soon. He has been so busy that the question of dealing with legal documents has been shelved for the time being.

Sadly, his son, Jason, has split up with his wife. She left him suddenly and is now nowhere to be found. Now Jason has to figure out how to juggle his job and parenting. He cannot afford day care, and his parents are still employed and therefore cannot be everyday caregivers.

In desperation, Jason calls his little sister in Ethiopia. As always, Kristin manages to calm him down. She reminds him about their cousin Sally, located just 100 miles from Jason. Sally lives in the country with her husband and three children, cows, pigs, dogs, chickens, and a vegetable garden the size of Texas. Maybe she is be willing to give a home to Jason's child for a little while, until he can save enough money to support the two of them.

Two weeks after this phone conversation, Kristin flies home for a quick briefing with her company. Her plane skids on an icy runway and crashes into an airport hangar. Kristin ends up in the hospital, unconscious. The doctors think she will regain consciousness shortly, but in the meantime, they need permission to operate on her punctured lung. Kristin's attorney-in-fact for health care, her father, is on hand and able not only to make treatment decisions, but also — with his wife's help — to make sure the hospital staff provides only the absolute best for their daughter. He notices that his opinion is taken seriously by everyone once they become aware he is Kristin's legal representative.

This chapter is about a few other forms that are often used in conjunction with POAs. These are the affidavit of attorney-in-fact and the revocation of POA. Other ancillary forms pertaining to POAs are not directly related to the power of attorney document, but often are signed at the same time or in the same spirit. Such forms include the living will, the do-not-resuscitate order, and the anatomical gifts form. In addition, the living trust is used in some states for comprehensive estate management.

Affidavit of Attorney-in-Fact

Unless revoked, POAs terminate upon the death of the principal. As the principal, you are free to revoke the powers you assign to another at any time. Therefore, it can happen that a creditor or other third party asks for assurance that your agent is still authorized to act in your place. In this situation, an affidavit of attorney-in-fact document is provided. This is simply a sworn statement by the attorney-in-fact that to the best of his or her knowledge, the POA document originally signed and giving the agent authority is still in effect and does not have to be revoked or declared invalid.

This form is notarized when the agent completes it and is legally recognized as assurance to others that decisions regarding your financial affairs or medical care still rest with the agent. You as principal are not involved in this assurance, and therefore it is wise to periodically review and, if necessary, update the status of whatever documents you have signed, as well as to be sure to revoke powers in a timely fashion. State law takes great pains to clarify when the powers of attorney-in-fact are in effect and almost always includes directives saying third parties must honor the decisions and actions of your agent. Sometimes, the law even spells out cases in which compensation for damages may be claimed if a third party refuses to honor your POA.

Revocation of POA

A POA should spell out the conditions under which the specifics contained within it are or are not in effect. Once the duties described have been carried out or the specified time has passed, the document automatically expires and becomes invalid.

However, at some point you may wish to revoke the privileges you have assigned in the POA due to illness, death, disagreement, or estrangement between you and your agent. You might simply change your mind about who should represent you. If a health care POA is involved, you may decide you want to take back your decision-making and not be represented by another. This is sometimes allowable, even though a physician has officially judged that you are incompetent. Regardless of the reason, you have the right to revoke the powers you have delegated.

State laws differ widely regarding how you can perform a revocation. Because the rights of the individual are at stake, the law usually tries to make it easy to revoke attorney-in-fact privileges. In some locations, it is sufficient to destroy the original POA document. In other places, it may be necessary to obtain a physician's certification that the principal has regained mental competence. Commonly, because the rights of the individual are at stake here, the law tries to make it incredibly easy to revoke attorney-in-fact privileges. But completing a written revocation of POA form is the safest approach.

Forms Relating to Health Care POAs

The remaining ancillary forms pertaining to POAs actually are not directly related to the power of attorney document, but often are signed at the same time or in the same spirit.

Thanks to the surge in aging baby boomers and new technology, a significant amount of attention has turned lately to preparations for old age. In addition, large numbers of our senior population are relatively healthy physically, but mentally incompetent due to Alzheimer's disease or other cognitive weakening associated with age. Our own love affair with physical fitness and healthy habits has resulted in our bodies outliving our minds.

Though making sure you complete the process of naming your personal representatives through POAs is the first step in dealing with your potential incapacity, other legal documents should cover most eventualities. These are the living will, DNR order, and anatomical gifts form.

Living will

The living will (also known by other names, including "advance directive") is a document that states your preferences for treatment when you are in a persistent vegetative state or irreversible, terminal condition due to an accident, illness, or other event. Various life-support measures can prolong life even if the patient has little hope of recovery. A living will can make your treatment wishes clear in such circumstances.

Would you want mechanical life support after falling into a persistent vegetative state? Would you want to be kept alive through the administration of water and nutrients? A living will allows you to state in advance your preferences regarding such treatment scenarios.

Your chosen representative may be named in this form as the person authorized to enforce your wishes, but the completed document itself is by and large respected as your official directive, with or without an agent. It important to note that in an actual medical emergency, the directives contained in the living will actually overrule any decisions your agent may make. At the end, it is your written statement that prevails, not the authority of your attorney-in-fact. While there are slight variations from state to state, all states should generally accept your properly prepared living will.

Beginning in 1990, the U.S. government began to officially allow people to express their wishes when it comes to the end of their own lives. Legally, medical professionals are obligated to follow the instructions found in a living will or advance health care directive, so long as the person was in a healthy and clear state of mind when signing the document. If you are diagnosed with a potentially terminal illness, or you suffer a debilitating accident, you may not be able to prepare your living will after your diagnosis or accident if your state of mind is legally determined to be impaired. This is a determination your physician can certify.

A durable health care POA can offer some of the same protections as a living will, especially if the attorney-in-fact is well-educated about the principal's preferences. However, a living will is often a good idea, as it is much safer to have written proof of your desires. It is more explicit than a POA. Should a court become involved in a final decision, written evidence in your own voice will carry weight.

In addition, medical personnel may be more inclined to preserve life at all costs, because that is their responsibility, and this could conflict with the directives of your attorney-in-fact. A statement that clearly comes from you as the principal is the safest way to guard against conflicting views. Also, because a living will does not cover all medical situations, a durable health care POA is a good addition to your planning documents.

You do not need to worry that your agent will be left alone to determine what state the principal is in. Most living wills have stipulations requiring that two doctors agree on the patient's state of health before delivering that information to the family members and agent.

Living wills also have other protections built into them that look out for everyone's best interests. They include detailed lists of instructions regarding treatment options, and a requirement that the doctor treating the patient must follow the instructions in the will — or, if they are unwilling to do so, they must transfer care of the patient to another physician who will follow the instructions detailed in the living will. The living will must also be entered into the patient's medical record.

While a living will signed in one state is likely to be honored in another, there are differences in living-will statutes from state to state. Some states use different terminology for the concept, such as "advance directive for health care" rather than "living will." Some state laws allow a living will to be submitted orally. Others allow for family members to give consent. If you spend a lot of time in more than one state, you may want to sign a living will for each state. This can make things simpler if the time should come to exercise your living will.

To make sure a living will is valid and legal, you must sign the document in front of two witnesses with whom there are no conflicts of interest. This means witnesses cannot be any of your doctors or other health care providers, heirs or relatives.

Take a copy of your living will to your doctors, hospital, or nursing home. Primary care physicians should have a copy of your wishes on file so that in an emergency, decisions can be made quickly.

DNR order

A do-not-resuscitate document is used in cases where the patient has a terminal disease or is otherwise nearing death. If a patient's heart stops beating or the lungs stop working, medical personnel are legally obligated to work to revive the patient. However, if you are terminally ill and suffering, you may prefer not be revived. A DNR order gives you that option.

The form is signed by you and a physician and kept in a place in your home where emergency medical personnel can easily access it. A DNR order should also be placed in the records department of your primary physician, hospital, and nursing home.

Anatomical gift form

The anatomical gift form is a simple statement that indicates your willingness upon death to donate organs or other body parts to medicine or for use in transplants. Many lives are saved through these gifts.

The form is often readily available upon admission to a hospital. Some states' driver's license application forms also offer this option. According to The National Conference of Commissioners on Uniform State Laws Web site, the Revised Uniform Anatomical Gift Act of 2006 has been adopted in 37 states, Washington, D.C., and the U.S. Virgin Islands, and in 2009, was introduced in five more states.

The Uniform Act includes suggested forms (called the "donor card") for your anatomical gifts. This form is a part of many wills and trusts.

You may be specific, choosing which body parts you wish to donate. To find out more about your options, visit the Uniform Act Web site at **www.anatomicalgiftact.org**.

Myths regarding anatomical gifts

This section details some of the common myths and misconceptions that prevent many people from allowing their organs to be donated. Many people prefer to preserve their body after death. If you have reservations regarding organ donation, do not feel guilty. The most important thing is that you feel at ease with your decisions.

However, if you are interested in organ donation, but have doubts regarding the treatment of your body or your organs, the following information may help to make up your mind.

Myth: **Agreeing to be an organ donor is the same as agreeing to subpar medical treatment.**
Many people worry that if it becomes known that they are willing to be an organ donor, then doctors will not work as hard to save their lives. This is simply not the case. Medical professionals are bound by ethical codes requiring them to look out for your best interests. Furthermore, the doctor treating you in the emergency room is not likely to oversee a patient's long-term care for kidney failure. There is little chance of conflict of interest.

Myth: **If I have my organs donated, my body will be destroyed, and I cannot have an open-casket funeral.**
You may feel that doctor's will have little concern with preserving your body while harvesting donated organs. However, organs need to be carefully extracted or else they will be unusable. Thus, doctors must be careful with the body when removing those organs. Also, people generally wear clothes during their funerals, which will conceal any evidence of organ removal. In other words, the removal of organs will most likely not signifi-

cantly alter a person's appearance or make an open-casket funeral impossible.

Myth: **I am too old/too young/not healthy enough to
donate organs.**

While the health of a person will certainly affect the quality of
many organs, due to the extensive list of organs and tissues that
can be donated, it is likely that at least some of your organs will
be able to be used. And while you may feel you are not in good
enough health to donate organs, a doctor will be able determine
that for sure. The decision is not made until the time your organs
are being considered for use.

Myth: **My organs will most likely go to rich people, not necessarily the people who are next in line.**

Even though celebrities and the rich generate more attention
when they receive an organ, or when they need one, they have
to wait in line like everyone else. People who need organs and
are waiting for organ donations are in a system called the United
Network for Organ Sharing. This system keeps the allocation of
organs ready for donations on track. There are more than 87,000
people in the system who are waiting for organ donations. It is
estimated that 17 people die daily while waiting for transplants.

Myth: **I may not be dead when they decide to take my organs.**

Sometimes people worry their organs will be harvested pre-
maturely. Families may question whether doctors should have
worked for a few more minutes before harvesting the organs.
When doctors decide to harvest a person's organs, it is clear that
person has died. In fact, people who have agreed to organ donation are put through additional tests to prove they are indeed

dead that those who have not decided to donate their organs are not put through.

Living trust

Trusts and their creation for the purpose of handling your affairs are outside the scope of this book, but it is appropriate to distinguish them from the POA. Living trusts may include financial and health care POAs, a living will, a last will and testament, and several other forms pertaining to life-succession planning. A trust is chiefly a way of managing larger amounts of money and assets, dealing effectively with taxation, and avoiding probate after death.

Your lawyer will likely recommend setting up a living trust if:

- Your wealth is at a level that would benefit from the protections offered through a trust.

- Your prospects and affairs are sufficiently complex to warrant the comprehensive protection involved in a trust.

- You want to transfer ownership of your assets to another person or institution.

If so, all the necessary and desired POAs will be included in the trust-making process. Note that a trust is not a do-it-yourself process, and — unlike a simple stand-alone POA — you will need to enlist the services of an attorney to create one, preferably one who is a specialist in this area of law.

The living trust is a large and complicated document, custom-made for you by your attorney, and so there is no sample document included in this book. We will, however, discuss some of the advantages, difficulties, and instructions for assembling a living trust.

Your estate is the total of your possessions and holdings. The person who will settle your estate if you do not appoint a person yourself is called the administrator. A court can appoint this person based on evidence and testimony; however, the court may or may not understand what it is that you would have wanted.

You will need to select one or more beneficiaries to receive the various items in your estate. You can name one beneficiary and leave all that you have to that person. Or, you can divide your estate among as many beneficiaries as you wish. You can also name a charity, organization, or business entity as your beneficiary and leave your estate to it.

Your beneficiaries may or may not be actual heirs. Heirs are people who — without other stipulations outlined in a will or living trust — would receive the estate or the pieces of the estate upon a principal's death. Heirs are defined by state statute.

You may also consider an alternative beneficiary. This is a person who can accept the part of the estate you leave to a beneficiary if that first-named beneficiary is unable to receive your estate for a situation spelled out by you in the trust, or if the beneficiary dies before receiving the estate.

If you do not name beneficiaries, the courts will distribute your assets in a certain pattern defined by law. The first in line will be your spouse, whether in whole or in part, which is generally dependent on whether you also have children. If you are not married, the next people in line to receive your estate will be your children. If you have no children, the estate then generally passes to your parents. If they are already deceased, your brothers and sisters are usually next in line. In some states, grandparents stand in close proximity in inheritance. It depends on the state's priority of heirs. Eventually, if no heirs in the hierarchy can be found, the estate passes to the state itself.

While this makes sense legally, as there must be an orderly resolution of dispersal of property, it does not necessarily follow a logical emotional line in individual cases. Further, there is the still-changing arena of civil unions and same-sex marriage relationships, which may not be recognized by your state's laws. Or, you may be in a long-term relationship that is, for all intents and purposes, a marriage — but without the legal document or supporting state law declaring it so. Only some states recognize "common law" marriages.

You should also consider that taking care of someone else's estate is a lot of work. Perhaps the beneficiary you have chosen is simply not in a condition to take care of your affairs. Maybe they are dealing with extended family situations of their own, or are sick or disabled themselves.

You can deal with such unwanted eventualities in one of two ways, or a combination of them: a properly drafted last will and testament and a living trust. Creating a living trust will help alleviate any undue stress and will prevent your estate from falling to someone who is not equipped to take care of it.

One of the most important people involved in your last will and testament or your living trust is your personal representative. This is the person who — like your attorney-in-fact for POA appointments — will make sure your wishes are upheld when you die. There are two types of personal representatives. The person who makes sure the items in your will are carried out properly is your executor. The person you name to handle overseeing the execution of your trust is called your successor trustee.

Revocable living trust

You may choose to have a living trust that is revocable. This means the principal, or grantor, has the option to change the arrangements of the trust, or even cancel it altogether, at any time. This situation can be helpful if you want to see if a person will be the kind of beneficiary you want to inherit any part of your estate. If a beneficiary begins spending money unwisely in the grantor's opinion, the grantor can change his or her mind about having that person as a benefactor, or can set standards the benefactor has to reach before being allowed to receive their portion of the estate. With a revocable living trust, the owner of the trust can put the trust into action and see if it is working the way he or she would like it to.

One more concern to keep in mind with a revocable living trust is that the grantor of the trust must continue to monitor and work with the trust. If you, as the grantor of your living trust, transfer assets to a bank or another holder of part of the estate, you must make sure to watch how that entity manages your assets.

Last will and testament

A last will and testament is a document people use to explain their wishes for belongings and assets upon death. It is best to write a will when you are in good health and in a positive state of mind. Writing your will before it is needed will allow you to think through your decisions instead of making hurried decisions in the heat of a stressful moment.

We should also note that a will differs from a living will in that a living will gives instructions for managing the care of a person while they are alive. A last will gives instructions for what to do with a person's property when he or she is dead.

The language of a will

Television — especially soap operas — has made people at least somewhat familiar with the dramatic-sounding words entailed in the lines, "I, John Doe, being of lawful age and of sound mind..."

While this makes for fun and interesting storytelling, these words actually have a very real purpose. As a legal document, it is important for the will to declare that the person creating the document has the mental capacity to do so. The language at the beginning of a will simply makes this clear.

This language will also say something to the effect of: "...under no restraint, do hereby revoke all other wills and codicils."

These are two important phrases. The first one ("under no restraint") explains that this document is being written with the writer's consent, and that no one is forcing him or her to do this.

This stipulation is important to note because forcing someone to write a will could be an extremely manipulative situation and could effectively make the will invalid.

The second phrase ("do hereby revoke all other wills and codicils") is a bit redundant, but important nonetheless. This statement makes sure there is no confusion about which will is controlling, should there be any prior wills. In some states, a new will automatically revokes prior wills; in others, a prior will is revoked only to the extent that it is different. Therefore, it is best to be very clear that the new will revokes all prior wills. If this were not the case, mass confusion could be created in families as members, heirs, and potential beneficiaries tried to sort out which version of the will was the most current or most correct. Installing language into a will stating that the most current version is the one that should be adhered to clears up this issue and makes it possible to move forward with the deceased's wishes with confidence and without confusion.

The introductory section of the will contains a few more declarations. The will states:

- Your name and where you live
- The date
- Language that this document is a will
- The name of the person you want to act as your executor
- The name of a person you select to be your alternative executor
- The name of the person or names of people you want to serve as guardians to your children or other dependants

for whom you care

- The name of person or names of people you want to serve as successor guardians to your children or other dependants for whom you care

- Sections stating with whom you wish to leave your assets. These statements are called "bequests"

- Your wishes for your care after you have died — your funeral, burial or cremation arrangements, and so on. You can also include in this section if you do not wish to have a service at all

- Your signature, followed by the names and places of residence of at least two witnesses who observed you signing the document

- The seal of a notary public, if your state requires it

There are several different types of will. They include:

- **Reciprocal or mutual will**: The reciprocal will is a tool for married couples who intend to leave their assets to each other. Each member of the couple fills out a will. The wills are identical — save for the switching of the names. Check with your state to find out if changes made to one will automatically are reflected in the other, or if you need to make the changes to both documents.

- **Holographic will**: A holographic will is one written by hand and signed but not verified by witnesses. These are valid documents in some states.

- **Pour-over will into a trust**: A pour-over will is a document that looks out for property that has not been assigned to a beneficiary after a principal's death, or that you may wish to delay the dispersal to a beneficiary directly.

With a pour-over clause in our last will and testament, the property is put into ("poured over" into) a trust that will hold and administer it according to the terms you have set up for the trust. In some cases, a principal has acquired a piece of property close to the time of his or her death and simply did not have the time or resources to rework the paperwork already included in his or her living trust. He or she can name the trust as the beneficiary in the will to receive the property.

It is also a way of putting property into the trust at the time of your death that you did not wish to, or could not, put into the trust during your lifetime. But whatever the reason, a pour-over provision in your will allows you this method of adding property at the time of our death to the living trust you had previously established.

CASE STUDY: POAS — A FAMILY AFFAIR

Pam Whitaker
Baton Rouge, LA

My husband and I chose our two children to be co-executors. They are the only two heirs at this time, and they both share equally. We are close to our children and feel they would make their decisions based on our wishes and their love for each other.

My husband's parents and my parents did the same thing. Executing my mother's estate with my brother was simple and avoided any resentment that might have come with only one of us having been chosen.

My mother had a living will and gave me power of attorney over any health issues, since I lived close to her. When she decided to draw up a living will, I went with her. My brother was too upset with the idea of my mother's death to participate. Maybe it is a female thing, but preparing for everything life unfailingly brings to us seemed practical. I was certainly emotional, but mother felt supported and confident, and also knew she was caring for her children. We had the opportunity to discuss not only her estate, but my own. Obviously, one day I would die and want someone to take care of my children.

My two children were a little uncomfortable with the idea that their mom and stepfather would be kicking the bucket, but I think they were honored and pleased that we trusted them with such a personal responsibility.

I can tell you about my feelings being chosen as co-executor for my mother's estate. Initially, my mother chose only my brother as both executor and heir because she thought he would make the best financial decisions.

One day, my mother, sister-in-law, and I were talking about divorce. My sister-in-law made the statement that if my brother ever divorced her, she would take him for every penny he had. She said she knew the judges and lawyers in the town where she grew up and currently lived.

It was a statement women often make to other women and was not based on any trouble in their marriage — just one of those comments made at the wrong time in the company of the wrong people.

I did not think much about it, but two weeks later my mother changed her will, giving us equal shares, and naming my brother and me as co-executors. Soon after that, my brother and I became closer, and after years of getting to know one another, we are close. None of it was about the money my mother left us — only about being family.

This Is A Lot Of Work — Do I Really Need To Worry?

The short answer is yes. You will be doing a bit of work, but it will save you and your family an amazing amount of stress later on. The saying goes that an ounce of prevention is worth a pound of cure, and that statement is no less true when it comes to taking care of these types of affairs.

You cannot afford to die

One issue that will arise immediately upon your death or incapacitation is how expensive your life is. Whether you have passed away or cannot communicate because you are in a persistent vegetative state or a coma, the pieces of your life that cost money will still need attention. Credit card bills will need to be paid. Your rent or mortgage check will need to go to the landlord or the bank. Your children will have school costs that need to be managed. If you have a pet, the animal will need to be fed, housed, and tended to. Your car payment will still need to be taken care of. There may be hospital bills and, eventually, funeral costs. A stay in an intensive care unit can cost hundreds, if not thousands, of dollars a day. According to the Federal Trade Commission's Web site, "a traditional funeral, including a casket and vault, costs about $6,000, although 'extras' like flowers, obituary notices, acknowledgment cards, or limousines can add thousands of dollars to the bottom line. Many funerals run well over $10,000." Someone must manage these accounts and concerns.

Without some direction about financial resources, you run the risk of defaulting on loans, losing your assets, and having your estate fall into someone else's hands or ruin. You may think that wills, living wills, and trusts only need to come into play if you have large amounts of wealth. This is not the case. Even if you do not have a large amount of assets, the things you do own have value to you, and you will want them to be taken care of if you cannot take care of them yourself. A POA can ensure that the things in your life that you consider valuable are given the care they deserve. If you have money you have set aside for emergencies but no one knows that it exists, you may cause your family undue debt and anxiety because they do not know there is money available to help them take care of you.

Not making plans for your assets — and making those plans and wishes known — may cause you to fall prey to the court system. Court proceedings can take years to complete. By the time your estate has been settled, feelings may have been hurt beyond repair and assets depleted. In order to ease tensions and make the value of your property as high as possible, you will need to make plans for managing your assets before the need arises.

The word intestate means to die without a will. If you die intestate, the court will make all the decisions regarding where your money and property goes according to state law. There is very little discretion involved.

Each state handles the issue of someone dying intestate in its own way, and the state's way may or may not be *your* way.

To Review:

Although your POA documents are important, there are many other supplemental documents needed as well. Each form or document helps support your life and your end-of-life decisions in a different way.

Livings wills and DNR forms both relate to procedures that can be used to save your life or allow it to naturally end if you should be in an accident or suffer from a debilitating illness. Both of these forms let doctors and other medical professionals know which procedures you would like performed — or not — in any of these situations. Medical professionals are bound to observe your wishes — as long as they know what your wishes are. Once you prepare these documents, you will need to give copies to your primary care physician and family members so they are readily accessible to doctors who may attend to you in a time of crisis.

By filling out an anatomical gift form, you can arrange to have your body — organs and tissues — donated to others who may need them. Some people worry that if they agree to be an organ donor, doctors will not work as hard to save their lives if they should come into a hospital following an accident. This is one belief that prevents many people from agreeing to be organ donors. But unless you have stated otherwise in a DNR or living will, a doctor will do everything he or she can to keep you alive — whether you are an organ donor or not.

Wills and living trusts are also important parts of your end-of-life planning. Living trusts are comprehensive documents that may encompass your living will or advance directives, last will and testament, living or pour-over trusts, POAs, and DNR form.

It is easy to think that because there are so many forms to fill out, it may not be worth the effort. But if you were to die without much of this paperwork in place, you could leave your family in chaos, compounded by grief. If you die without a will in place, the courts will take the responsibility of divvying up your estate according to statute. And while the court system will follow laws and procedures, they cannot possibly take into account the nuance of personal relationships that exist among your family members. You are in a much better position to determine who will take the best care of your estate than the court system.

Chapter 8

Working with an Attorney to Prepare Your POA

MEET THE JONESES

The year in the lives of the Jones family is nearly at an end. George did encounter the need to prove his POA document was still in effect, as the trim carpenter did not know him and so questioned his authority to direct the job. George had signed an affidavit of attorney-in-fact and produced the document, which served to reassure the suspicious carpenter. On the whole, George is pleased with his decision to take on the job. Now that it is over, he is back home. It is time to get down to that advance directive business.

Having had the experience of advocating for Kristin during his daughter's recent medical trauma, George and Diane are anxious to cover their own bases in these respects. Kristin is doing fine and is back on the job, full-tilt. Her brother, Jason, has much to be proud of as well. He gave his cousin Sally power of attorney for childcare while she graciously hosted Jason's son for three months. During that time, Jason figured out how to capitalize on his botanical expertise and now has a decent income from a gardening Web site he established. The venture supplements the income he earns from his landscaping job. He is almost ready to support his child at home, and the prospect fills him with hope.

George and Diane want to shield their offspring from difficulties that may arise as the couple ages. They also want to make the right choices about the future. They know that completing an advance directive includes naming an attorney-in-fact and discussing a range of other issues related to how they will spend their final days. They also need to plan for what will happen to their assets when they no longer are able to tend to them.

They would feel most comfortable discussing all this with a professional, so George and Diane make an appointment with an attorney Diane found through diligent Internet research.

In many cases, you can successfully and legally complete a POA without hiring an attorney. If you are clear about the tasks you wish your attorney-in-fact to perform and which form of the document to use, you may be fine going it on your own.

However, consider consulting a lawyer if you have a lot of assets, your affairs are complicated, or you are simply confused about the process. Establishing a relationship with an attorney can be helpful, especially for clients in middle age or beyond. An attorney can become familiar with a client's wishes and help set up protections for old age. Such an attorney will be well-prepared to defend the client if challenges arise.

Locating an Attorney

Because many people do not necessarily rub elbows with attorneys in their daily lives, you may be somewhat at a loss when it comes to selecting one you are comfortable with. Of course, the phone book is full of names, and there are countless attorney Web sites on the Internet, but how do you know whom you can trust and with whom you can work well?

One way to go about locating a lawyer is to ask friends and neighbors about their experiences. Chances are high that someone you trust and respect can recommend a good lawyer or firm.

A specialist in estate planning is typically the best choice. Most lawyers have a grasp of the basic issues of the law, but a lawyer's specialty plays a big part in whether or not he or she will be able to help you. Several states use a process of testing and credentialing to certify lawyers as estate and probate specialists.

State bar associations typically offer referral services, and you often can find attorneys in your area by searching the state bar Web site. FindLaw (**www.findlaw.com**) also can help you find a lawyer or POA forms specific to your state.

When interviewing prospective attorneys, ask if the firm often handles POA documents — not just in their creation, but in conjunction with transactional work. Ask how much the lawyer charges to prepare a POA and how long the process will take.

Other questions to ask include:

- How long have you been practicing?
- Where are you licensed to practice?
- What portion of your work includes preparing POAs and estate planning?
- Are there any "hidden" charges?

Working with the Attorney

Reading through this handbook will help arm you with the questions to ask and issues to discuss.

Do not be afraid to ask the attorney a lot of questions. If you do not clearly understand the responses, ask again. As the client, you have the right to be fully aware of and understand all that is involved.

You can be perfectly frank with your attorney, as he or she is legally bound to keep your information confidential. Do not withhold information, even if it may not seem directly relevant, as all factors are to be considered when completing your document.

In some cases, the process may take longer than you would have hoped. You can speed things up by staying in touch. If you do not hear from the attorney when you expect to, give him or her a call. Ask what you can do to help or when you can expect the next step to be completed. Establishing a friendly relationship with the secretary or paralegal at the firm is a good idea and can ensure you get the proper attention.

Your work with the attorney will be more successful if you are fully prepared before meetings and phone calls. Learn all you can about POAs, including the different kinds that exist and which type is appropriate for you. Decide in advance who will serve as your attorney-in-fact and discuss the assignment with that person to be sure you have their consent. Also, identify one or two others who can be named as alternatives.

If you have worked out your needs in advance and can communicate them to the attorney, the process may require no more than one meeting at the attorney's office to complete the signing, witnessing, and notarizing of the POA. In this case, the lawyer's fee is minimal, and you have created a relationship with the professional that could come in handy down the line.

If you do work with a lawyer, witnesses and a notary will be supplied as part of the process.

Making Sure the Relationship Works

It can be easy when someone is in a position of power or is more proficient in a subject to assume any doubts you have are unfounded and unimportant. This is not the case when it comes to planning your POA. You know more about your life than the attorney — even if he or she went to law school, and you did not.

You can do the preplanning and ask the proper questions and still end up with an attorney who is not the right fit for you. Granted, the process for preparing a POA is not particularly long, but you may have questions down the road or need to make changes to the documents that will require the continued help of your lawyer. Also, if there are any disputes from the person with whom the agent is interacting, your lawyer may be a helpful person to contact to ease any tension. It is important to be able to easily get all the information you need. When asking questions of a lawyer, you should get helpful answers. If you feel awkward asking questions or do not get timely and helpful answers, the attorney may not be the best choice for you.

There are many reasons why a lawyer might be slow to answer questions. Many attorneys take on large case loads and may not have the time. It is also possible that the attorney is less vested in your case because it is short and consists of fewer billable hours. If you do not get the attention you deserve, look elsewhere.

As we have discussed, many of the decisions you will make regarding your POA and choice of agent are very personal. Many legal issues raise religious, philosophical, and spiritual considerations. A lawyer should allow you to make these decisions on your own. He or she should discuss the legal implications of your decisions but should not make decisions for you.

You may come to your attorney with any version of your POA wishes in place. Perhaps you have the forms completed and need a final review, or maybe you have just begun the process and are still trying to sort it all out. Whatever stage of the process you are in, and whatever your final decisions are, make sure you are the one making them. If the attorney crosses the line between providing professional and legal advice and making personal decisions for you, reassert your boundaries and consider looking for representation elsewhere.

Finally, your documents should be sound and trouble-free. If you find that the POA documents have errors, or if a medical professional or financial institution is unable to use them, look for an attorney who can get it right.

POA forms are used by lay people, so there should be relatively little expert work required from a lawyer. Because this is a fairly simple transaction, any significant errors are reason for concern.

CASE STUDY: USING AN ATTORNEY TO PREPARE YOUR POA

Rick Kent
Los Angeles

As a paralegal, I worked with a man whose mother had been of diminished mental capacity and had died. He needed the POA to make decisions with her money and real estate. He needed to sell her home and distribute her money.

I think people should avoid drafting their own legal documents because it can be tricky. Wording is very intricate and will be scrutinized. If something is off by one word, which the layperson would not necessarily notice, the whole purpose could be defeated. "Legalese" is its own language. Words can have one meaning in general conversation, but mean something completely different in a legal document.

More importantly, a legal document prepared by a trained professional should cover every possible contingency that would protect the rights of the person on whose behalf it is being drafted. An untrained person, doing it alone, could easily leave something out that might protect his or her interests.

People who draft their own documents may lack protection due to key errors or omissions, or a do-it-yourselfer might include something in a document that is not allowable by law. In a worst-case scenario, a layperson could conceivably be open to an action against him or her for practicing law without a license.

Firing an Attorney

Despite your best preparations and precautions, you may still have an unsatisfactory experience with your chosen attorney. Perhaps the process is taking entirely too long (several months is far more than required for this relatively simple document); perhaps the attorney seems too aloof or impatient with your questions; perhaps your situation changes, and you decide to work with someone else for any reason.

At any time, you can fire an attorney. It is a good idea to provide notice in writing, although a phone call can get the ball rolling. Ask the attorney's office for any personal information and other documents in your file. The attorney will keep his or her notes and any work in progress, but you are entitled to have all your own papers, as well as any documents or copies of completed documents you have requested and for which you have paid.

You will, of course, be liable for any bills you have incurred to date from the lawyer.

To Review:

While resources like this book will equip you to handle drafting your own POA and many other legal documents, you may wish to enlist the help of an attorney. If you do so, you should interview attorneys who are specialists in this area to make sure you find the one who is the best fit for you. You should also take care to recognize whether or not your attorney is working for you. When working with an attorney, you have the benefit of knowing that a professional is giving you professional-level advice, but you also have the professional-level expense.

Because of that expense, you should be sure you are getting advice and not being told what to do on a personal level. Your attorney is there to advise you about your options and how your decisions will be affected or permitted by the law — not to dictate what the right decision is for you.

Chapter 9

Specific State Laws

MEET THE JONESES

At the attorney's office, Diane and George Jones learn their state law allows them to select the forms to use in creating their advance directives. The attorney also explains the option of setting up a living trust. George is amazed at all the choices, and Diane is glad they decided to enlist the lawyer's aid. In the end, though, it is not so hard. After their first meeting at the law firm, the couple returns once again to sign the documents; then, it is done.

Meanwhile, because Kristin believes everything happens for a reason, she decides the plane crash is a sign she should slow down a little. Using her considerable influence at the pharmaceutical company, she lands a management position that allows her to stay in one location. At a street fair, she strikes up a conversation with a young architect and, after a whirlwind romance, they decide to get married next summer. Kristin plans to revoke the medical POA her father holds and execute a new one giving authority to her husband. This does not offend George in the slightest; he knows the stress of making decisions about someone else's bodily health.

Jason and his son are also doing well. The child enjoys day care, and he and his dad are very close. Jason has completed a durable health care POA — with Kristin as his attorney-in-fact.

The Joneses are a normal family, experiencing some good and some not-so-good times. They have had the wisdom and motivation to overcome problems proactively, and by setting up a few simple legal proofs, they have guarded themselves. They each take the time to reconsider and review their directives at least annually, so everything is kept up-to-date. Having prepared these documents, they are well-positioned for a "happily ever after."

The laws, forms, and requirements pertaining to POAs vary from state to state. Although the basic idea is the same everywhere, it is always best to use the forms provided by your particular state legislature when they exist. These are called *statutory* forms and are created by your lawmakers. While individual state laws frequently recommend this form, many states also allow for the use of other forms according to the citizen's wishes.

By using official state forms, everyone you are likely to encounter in exercising the POA will be familiar with the look and language of the forms. As a result, fewer questions are likely to be asked when these forms are used.

It is possible to use a different form — one that is either more generic or customized — that works well. Just make sure the document covers all the bases found in the statutory form.

A few states do not provide statutory forms at all, while others provide forms for some types of POAs but not others. In addition, states vary in several other respects regarding POAs. There may be laws addressing:

- Who is eligible to serve as an attorney-in-fact
- How many witnesses are required for the document signing

- The particulars of the *notary block* on the document, if required
- Third-party acceptance of the POA as valid
- Recourse for the principal if a third party rejects a valid POA

Most states (as well as the District of Columbia and the U.S. Virgin Islands) have adopted the Uniform Power of Attorney Act. This act establishes a standard POA form to be used in the states that have adopted the Act.

Only two states — Louisiana and Illinois — have not adopted the Uniform Power of Attorney Act. If you live in these states, you will not be able to use a standard form and have to create your own.

If your state does not have a standard durable POA form in its statutes, you may use the generic form included in this book's appendix. If you have any concerns, check with legal counsel.

Some statutory forms may have you indicate the powers you are giving to the agent by adding a check mark or your initials next to the desired powers. Other forms may have you cross out, check, or initial to show which powers you are *not* giving to the agent. This is an important distinction. In the first type of form, the agent will have only the powers you specify with the appropriate marking. In the second type of form, the agent will have *all* the powers listed on the form *except* for those marked. Make sure you understand which form you are using.

The following states have statutory forms that allow agents to have only the powers specifically stated in the POA document:

- Arkansas
- California
- Colorado
- District of Columbia
- Minnesota
- Montana

- Wisconsin
- North Carolina
- New York
- New Mexico
- Nebraska

The following states have forms that give agents any and all powers except those indicated by the principal on the POA form:

- Alaska
- Connecticut

- Texas
- Illinois

Finally, the following states only provide statutory forms for *durable* POAs:

- Florida
- Louisiana
- Missouri
- New Hampshire

- Virginia
- Pennsylvania
- Oregon
- Ohio

To create other types of POAs in these states, you will need to create your own POA documents or forms recommended by legal counsel in your state.

Following are some of the POA particulars in each state. This listing is meant merely to serve as a quick reference for some of the similarities and differences in POA procedures among the states. Check with your state's specific laws when preparing a POA.

Alabama

- Statutory forms do not indicate whether the forms are springing or durable. Be sure to check with current law to make sure your interests are represented on your POA.

- Has statutory health care POA.

Alaska

- Has statutory shortened POA forms available.

- Has statutory POA forms that give agents all powers unless indicated otherwise.

- With regards to financial POA forms, the principal needs to cross out any powers he or she does not wish to give to the agent.

Arizona

- Has a form stipulating conditions for witnesses and notaries.

- Statutory forms do not indicate whether they are springing or durable. Be sure to check with current law to make sure your interests are represented on your POA.

Arkansas

- Has statutory shortened POA forms available.

- Statutory financial POA forms give agents the powers specified in the document (as opposed to the form that denies the agent the powers specified on the document).

California

- Has statutory shortened POA forms available.

- Statutory financial POA forms give agents the powers specified in the document (as opposed to the type that denies the agent the powers specified on the document).

- Has a statutory health care POA.

Colorado

- Has statutory shortened POA forms available.

- Statutory financial POA forms give agents the powers specified in the document (as opposed to the form that denies the agent the powers specified on the document).

Connecticut

- Has a statutory all-in-one POA.

- Has shortened statutory POA forms available.

- Has statutory POA forms that give agents all powers, unless indicated otherwise.

- Statutory financial POA forms give agents the powers specified in the document (as opposed to the form that denies the agent the powers specified on the document).

- Has a statutory health care POA.

- Has a combination health care POA and living will.

Delaware

- Has a statutory health care POA.

District of Columbia

- Has shortened statutory POA forms available.

- On the DC statutory form, initial the powers you want to grant your agent.

- Has statutory health care POA forms.

Florida

- Only provides for a durable financial POA. Does not provide for a springing POA.

- Has statutory health care POAs.

- State language refers to the agent as the "surrogate."

- Has a section in the health care POA document that lists who else will receive a copy of the document.

Georgia

- Has shortened statutory POA forms available.

- Regarding the financial POA form, principals must initial the powers they want their agents to have and strike out the powers that they do not want their agents to have.

- There is a section on the financial POA document where the agent must sign to show he or she has officially accepted appointment to that position.

- Has statutory health care POAs.

- In the health care POA, there is space for the principal to indicate whom he or she would like to serve as his or her guardian should the court decide it necessary to do so.

- The health care POA form requires sample signatures from agents to use as evidence should the authenticity of an agent's appointment be called into question.

Hawaii

- Statutory forms do not indicate whether they are springing or durable. Be sure to check with current law to make sure your interests are represented on your POA.

- Has statutory health care POAs.

- State language refers to the agent as the "surrogate."

Illinois

- Has shortened statutory POA forms available.
- Has forms that allow agents to have all the powers indicated on the POA unless the principal indicates otherwise.
- Principals must cross out any powers they do not want agents to have.
- Has statutory health care POAs.
- Has a form that is designed to be a fill-in-the-blank form.

Iowa

- Has statutory health care POAs.

Kansas

- Has statutory health care POAs.

Kentucky

- Does not have a statutory form for either financial or a health care POA.

Louisiana

- Does not have a statutory form for either financial or health care POA.
- Does not provide for springing POAs.

Maine

- Certain notices are required to be filed with the POA form, but the state does not provide a POA form.
- Has a statutory health care POA law.

Maryland

- Has statutory health care POAs.

Minnesota

- Has shortened statutory POA forms available.

- Statutory financial POA forms give agents the powers specified in the document (as opposed to the form that denies the agent the powers specified on the document).

- Principals must place an "x" next to the powers that they wish their agents to have.

- Has statutory health care POAs.

Mississippi

- Has statutory health care POAs.

Missouri

- State laws only provide for durable financial POAs.

- Does not have statutory health care or financial POA forms.

Montana

- Has shortened statutory POA forms available.

- Statutory financial POA forms give agents the powers specified in the document (as opposed to the type that denies the agent the powers specified on the document).

- POAs are effective immediately upon signing a durable POA.

Nebraska

- Has shortened statutory POA forms available.

- Statutory financial POA forms give agents the powers specified in the document (as opposed to the form that denies the agent the powers specified on the document).

- Principals must place an "x" next to the powers that they wish their agents to have.

- Has statutory health care POAs.

Nevada

- Statutory forms do not indicate whether they are springing or durable. Be sure to check with current law to make sure your interests are represented on your POA.

- Has statutory health care POAs.

New Hampshire

- State laws only provide for durable financial POAs.

- Has statutory health care POAs.

New Jersey

- Does not have statutory health care or financial POA forms.

New Mexico

- Has a statutory all–in-one POA.

- Has shortened statutory POA forms available.

- Statutory financial POA forms give agents the powers specified in the document (as opposed to the form that denies the agent the powers specified on the document).

- Principals must initial the powers they want to give their agents. You can give all powers by signing one particular line.

- Agents must also sign an affidavit that attests to the validity of the POA.

- Has statutory health care POAs.

New York

- Has shortened statutory POA forms available.

- Statutory financial POA forms give agents the powers specified in the document (as opposed to the form that denies the agent the powers specified on the document).

- Agents must sign affidavits attesting that they know the POA form to be valid. They must sign this when they use the POA document, not when they set up the arrangement with the principal.

- Has statutory health care POAs.

North Carolina

- Has shortened statutory POA forms available.

- Statutory financial POA forms give agents the powers specified in the document (as opposed to the form that denies the agent the powers specified on the document).

- Has statutory health care POAs.

North Dakota

- Has statutory health care POAs.

Ohio

- Does not have statutory health care or financial POA forms.
- Only provides for durable financial POAs.

Oklahoma

- Has statutory health care POAs.

- Principals must initial after each power they wish to give their agents.

Oregon

- Only provides for durable financial POAs.

- Has statutory health care POAs.

- Provides a provision for your agent to sign to show that they accept their appointment as your agent.

Pennsylvania

- Does not have statutory health care or financial POA forms.

- Only provides for durable financial POAs.

Rhode Island

- Has statutory health care POAs.

South Carolina

- Has statutory health care POAs.

South Dakota

- Does not have statutory health care or financial POA forms.

Tennessee

- Has shortened statutory POA forms available.

- Has statutory health care POAs.

Texas

- Has shortened statutory POA forms available.

- Statutory forms give agents all powers except for those specifically indicated by the principal.

- Principals must cross out any powers they do not wish to grant their agents.

- Has statutory health care POAs.

Utah

- Does not have statutory health care or financial POA forms.

- Statutory forms do not indicate whether they are springing or durable. Be sure to check with current law to make sure your interests are represented on your POA.

- Has statutory health care POAs.

Vermont

- Has statutory health care POAs.

Virginia

- Only provides for durable financial POAs.
- Has statutory health care POAs.

Washington

- Does not have statutory health care or financial POA forms.

West Virginia

- Has statutory health care POAs.

Wisconsin

- Has shortened statutory POA forms available.

- Statutory financial POA forms give agents the powers specified in the document (as opposed to the form that denies the agent the powers specified on the document).

- Principals must initial the powers they wish to give their agents.

- Has statutory health care POAs.

Wyoming

- Does not have statutory health care or financial POA forms.

Examine your state's statutes or codes. State legal entities regularly revise laws and codes, and a significant court case can lead to a change in the law. Sometimes a tragic accident or statewide emergency can lead lawmakers to find weak spots in the law that need revising or changing. In fact, by the time this book goes to print, some laws regarding POA documents may have changed.

Refer to the appendix for further information about where you can find details pertaining to your specific state.

Health care POAs are relatively recent developments, and each state has taken its own approach to these issues. In 1990, the Federal Patient Self-Determination Act was adopted, ensuring protection for patients and requiring health care facilities to inform patients of their right to make an advance directive.

The Uniform Health-Care Decisions Act was approved by Congress shortly thereafter, as proposed by the National Conference of Commissioners on Uniform State Laws. This federal law spells out rights regarding personal health care and advance directives, including the durable health care POA. So far, the standardized methods suggested by the Act have been adopted in a few states, although other states had already established their own guidelines by the time the Uniform Health-Care Decisions Act was introduced.

To
Review:

The laws differ slightly from state to state when it comes to what you can and cannot do regarding your POA documents. To make sure your POA (or other legal forms) will be honored in your state, it is imperative to review your state's laws. Otherwise, you may find yourself unable to have your agent do the work you intend. Some of the differences that exist among the states are listed in this book. In order to find others, you should consult your state's statutes or legal counsel.

Chapter 10

How to Research for Your State's POA Laws

E ach U.S. state has a body of laws, variously called the code of law or state statutes, that include laws regarding POAs.

Laws change all the time. A hardbound publication about state laws is likely to be out of date by the time you read it, and this is why it is crucial to research the most recent version of your state's code of law.

A librarian can help you find the pertinent sections of your state code. This information is available online as well, though depending on your state, the information may be easy or difficult to locate. Just as states have their own laws, they also have their own Web presences, and the accessibility and user friendliness of legislative Web sites vary tremendously. If you are persistent, though, you can eventually find the information you seek.

The FindLaw.com Web site has a page (**http://law.findlaw.com/ state-laws/all-states.html**) that provides links to the official statutes of each of the 50 states and District of Columbia.

Once again, you can easily and cheaply purchase forms specific to your state's laws at an office supply store or online. When you do this, though, you are entrusting the legalities to the usually anonymous originator of the form — who, in these cases, is fairly invisible. By studying state laws yourself, you are in a position to know if the commercially supplied form is adequate.

Of course, not everyone can endure the rigors of reading legislative legalese. If you would rather bypass this step, the best advice is to make a quick trip to an attorney's office instead. Because POAs are common and often uncomplicated, an attorney can serve your needs quickly and inexpensively. In the end, the cost is not much more than purchasing the forms yourself, and it certainly can save headaches and worries, as well as be tailored to your specific set of circumstances.

The following chart lists Web addresses for state legal codes as of this writing.

STATE	STATUTORY FINANCIAL POA FORM	DURABLE OR SPRINGING ALLOWED	STATUTORY HEALTH CARE POA FORM	URL AND LOCATION OF STATUTORY FORMS
Alabama	No	Either	Yes	www.legislature.state.al.us/ CodeofAlabama/1975/coatoc. htm Title 22, Chapter 8A, Section 4 (health care)
Alaska	Yes	Either	Yes	www.legis.state.ak.us/de-fault.htm Title 13, Chapter 26, Section 332 (combined form)

Arizona	Yes	Either	Yes	**www.azleg.state.az.us/Ari-zonaRevisedStatutes.asp** Section 14-5501 (durable) Section 36-3224 (sample health care)
Arkansas	Yes	Either	Living will only	**www.arkleg.state.ar.us** Section 28-68-402 (durable) Section 20-17-202 (living will)
California	Yes	Either	Yes	**www.leginfo.ca.gov/calaw. html** Probate Code Section 4401 (only hard copy is available for financial POA)) Probate Code Section 4701 (health care)
Colorado	Yes	Either	Living will only	**www.michie.com/colorado** Section 15-1-1302 (durable) Section 15-14-506 (health care)
Connecticut	Yes	Either	Yes	**www.cga.ct.gov/asp/menu/ Statutes.asp** Section 1-43 (financial) Section 19a-576 (health care)
Deleware	No	Either	Yes	**http://delcode.delaware.gov** Section 16-2505 (health care)
District of Columbia	Yes	Either	Yes	**www.lawsource.com/also/ usa.cgi?go=usm%26xdc** Section 21-2101 (durable) Section 21-2207 (health care)
Florida	No	Either	Yes	**www.flsenate.gov/statutes/ index.cfm** Title 54, Section 765-203 (health care)
Georgia	Yes	Either	Yes	**www.lexis-nexis.com/hottop-ics/gacode/default.asp** Section 10-6-142 (financial) Section 31-32-4 (health care)
Hawaii	No	Either	Yes	**www.capitol.hawaii.gov/ site1/hrs/default.asp** Section 327e-16 (health care)
Idaho	No	Either	Yes	**www3.state.id.us/idstat/TOC/ idstTOC.html** Section 39-4510 (health care)

Illinois	Yes	Either	Yes	**www.ilga.gov/legislation/ilcs/ ilcs.asp** 755 ICLS 45/3-3 (short form POA for property law) 755 ICLS 45/4-10a (health care)
Indiana	No	Either	Living will only	**www.in.gov/legislative/ic/ code** Title 16, Article 36-4-10 (living will)
Iowa	No	Either	No	**www.legis.state.ia.us/index. html** The code includes suggested verbiage but not an actual form.
Kansas	No	Either	Yes	**www.kslegislature.org/leg- srv-statutes/getStatute.do** Section 58-632 (health care)
Kentucky	No	Either	Yes	**http://lrc.ky.gov/krs/titles.htm** Section 311.625 (health care)
Louisiana	No	Auto- matically durable un- less stated otherwise	Living will Only	**www.legis.state.la.us** Title 40, Section 1299.58.3 (living will)
Maine	No	Either	Yes	**http://janus.state.me.us/le- gis/statutes** Title 18-A, Section 5-804
Maryland	No	Auto- matically durable un- less stated otherwise	Yes	**www.michie.com/maryland** Health-General, Section 5-603 (health care)
Massachu- setts	No	Either	No	**www.mass.gov/legis/laws/ mgl**
Michigan	No	Either	No	**www.legislature.mi.gov**
Minnesota	Yes	Either	Yes	**www.revisor.leg.state.mn.us/ revisor/pages/statute** Chapter 523.23 (financial) Chapter 145C.16 (health care)
Mississippi	No	Either	Yes	**www.michie.com/mississippi** Title 41, Chapter 41-209 (health care)

Missouri	No	Auto-matically non-durable unless titled or stated otherwise	Living will only	**www.moga.mo.gov/STAT-UTES/STATUTES.HTM** Title 21, Section 459.015 (living will)
Montana	Yes	Durable only	Yes	**http://data.opi.state.mt.us/bills/mca_toc/index.htm** Title 72, Chapter 31-201 (financial) Title 50, Chapter 9-103 (health care)
Nebraska	Yes	Either	Yes	**http://uniweb.legislature.ne.gov** Section 49-1522 (financial) Section 30-3408 (health care)
Nevada	No	Either	Yes	**www.leg.state.nv.us/NRS** Section 449.830 (health care)
New Hampshire	Yes	Durable only	Yes	**www.gencourt.state.nh.us/rsa/html/indexes/default.html** Section 506:6 (durable) Section 137-J:20 (health care)
New Jersey	No	Either	No	**http://lis.njleg.state.nj.us**
New Mexico	Yes	Either	Yes	**www.conwaygreene.com/nmsu** Chapter 46B-1-301 (financial) Chapter 24-7A-4 (health care)
New York	Yes	Separate forms for durable, nondurable, and spring-ing POA	Yes	**http://public.leginfo.state.ny.us** General Obligations, Title 15, Section 5-1501 (financial) Public Health, Article 29-C-2981 (health care)
North Caroilna	Yes	Either	Yes	**www.ncga.state.nc.us** Chapter 32A-1 (financial) Chapter 32A-25 (health care)
North Dakota	No	Either	Yes	**www.legis.nd.gov/informa-tion/statutes/cent-code.html** Title 23, Chapter 06.5-17 (health care)
Ohio	No	Auto-matically durable un-less stated otherwise	Yes	**http://codes.ohio.gov/orc/1337**

Oklahoma	Yes	Either	Yes	**www.oscn.net/applications/ oscn** Title 15, Chapter 24.1003 (15-1003) (financial) Title 63, Chapter 60.3103.4 (60-3101.4) (health care)
Oregon	No	Durable unless limits are specified	Yes	**www.leg.state.or.us/ors** Chapter 12, Section 531 (health care)
Pennsylvania	Yes	Durable unless otherwise stated Also required forms for notice and acceptance by agent	A sample health care POA is suggested, not required	**www.pacode.com** Title 20, Chapter 56.01 (financial) Title 20, Chapter 54.71 (health care)
Rhode Island	Yes	Either	Yes	**www.rilin.state.ri.us/Statutes/ Statutes.html** Title 18, Chapter 16.2 (financial) Title 23, Chapter 4.10 (health care)
South Carolina	No	Either	Yes	**www.scstatehouse.net/code/ statmast.htm** Title 62, Chapter 5-504(D) (health care)
South Dakota	No	Either	No	**http://legis.state.sd.us/statutes/index.aspx**
Tennessee	No	Either	No	**www.michie.com/tennessee**
Texas	Yes	Either	Yes	**http://www.statutes.legis. state.tx.us** Probate Code, Chapter 12, Section 490 (financial) Health and Safety Code, Chapter 166, Section 164 (health care)
Utah	No	Nondurable unless otherwise stated	Yes	**www.le.ut.gov/~code/code. htm** Title 75, Chapter 02A.117 (health care)
Vermont	No	Either	No	**www.leg.state.vt.us/statutes/ statutes2.htm**
Virginia	No	Either	Yes	**http://leg1.state.va.us** Title 54.1, Chapter 29.84 (health care)

Washington	No	Either	Living will and mental health advance directive	**http://apps.leg.wa.gov/rcw** Title 70, Chapter 122.030 (living will) Title 71, Chapter 32.260 (mental health advance directive)
West Virginia	No	Either	Yes	**www.legis.state.wv.us/WV-CODE/Code.cfm** Chapter 16, Article 30.4 (health care)
Wisconsin	Yes	Either	Yes	**www.legis.state.wi.us/rsb/stats.html** Chapter 243.1(1) (financial) Chapter 155.30(2) (health care)
Wyoming	No	Either	No	**http://legisweb.state.wy.us/statutes/statutes.aspx**

Finding Additional Information

Although reading this book is a wise choice, and you may feel confident enough to move forward with your power of attorney and other legal-document decisions, you may still wish to know more. If this is the case, further research on the subject can be beneficial. Because these legal forms are so important to you and your family, you will want to make sure your research is as effective as possible. We will now look at a few ways to assist your efforts to find out more about the legal documents you may wish to prepare.

Why People Get it Wrong

The idea of doing research is not one of the more exciting things people can do with their spare time. The image of spending hours in a library, pouring over thick books or filtering through hundreds of hits on an Internet search is more boring than inspiring. But research is necessary to get the specific legal information that you require. To understand how to effectively research a subject, it is important to understand why people often get it wrong.

Research is boring

One of the main reasons people find research difficult to complete is because people tend to think research is boring, tedious work. Instead of lamenting over the amount of work ahead of you, realize that you are finding answers to your problems by being your own detective. The work you are doing to find the information to satisfy your legal needs is for your benefit. So approach research with an optimistic attitude. If this is not enough to inspire your detective nature, remember that by doing research on your own, instead of hiring an attorney, you are saving yourself from paying expensive legal fees. Even if you intend to utilize an attorney, knowing something about the process yourself in advance will streamline the process and save you time and money.

People do not know what they want

There is a wealth of information available online for you to find and use. This information overload can lead to stress when it comes to doing research. Once you start looking up information on a topic, it can be intimidating and daunting to sort through it all.

One of the best ways to avoid this problem is to know specifically what you need in your research. Make a list of the questions you want answered. By this point in this book, you probably have a good idea of what you need. Make a list of specific issues for which you need more information. For example, by this point, you should not need to research general power of attorney information, but maybe simply the details of how a POA works in Ohio. Maybe you just need to find the right attorney. Streamline what you are looking for and searching for your answers will be much easier.

Break the Spine

Despite the challenges of research, the following are ways to find information easily to help you find the remaining knowledge you need to complete your POA, advance directive/living will, DNR order, or living trust.

Take a look at this book. What state are the pages in, now that you are almost at the end? If there are no dog-eared pages and highlighted areas, or if the spine of the book is still intact, then go back and make a bit of a mess. Reading can be a very passive activity; it is easy to flip through page after page and not really absorb the content.

To make sure you note the information that is pertinent to your situation, pick up a pen or highlighter, crack the spine of your book, and really get into the pages. Unless a friend has let you borrow this book, it belongs to you, so make it yours. Highlight important passages, words you do not understand, or concepts about which you would like to find more information. Highlighting or underlining can make it easier for you to remember certain pieces of information. It will also make it easier for you when you are looking back through the book to find the information most pertinent to your case.

Take a holistic approach

Every issue is made up of many smaller issues that combine together into one large system. As we have seen in this book, creating the right POA for you involves understanding familial relationships; communication and learning styles; various medical treatments and procedures; and, of course, the law itself.

Therefore, if you approach your research from only one angle, you may find yourself coming up short in terms of what you really need to know. You must make sure to examine all angles of whatever it is that you are researching to arrive at a complete answer that fulfills your needs.

Also, once you complete your POA, living will, DNR, or trust, you will need to keep up with legal, family, and social issues to make sure your wishes are continuing to be met. You can do this by keeping yourself abreast of news and current events. The Terry Schiavo case brought a lot of attention to end-of-life issues. Following current events can help you make sure you are aware of the nuances that affect laws and issues that affect your own philosophies.

Advances in medicine and new philosophies developed through professional research can alter what doctors and other medical professionals consider proper hospital policy. Religious groups can put pressure on lawmaker to bend public policy to their agendas and desires. Other advocacy groups also have a lot of sway and influence lawmakers on both the national and local level.

While it is impossible to get to know every group that may have lobbyists helping to promote their wishes, it is fairly easy to find ways of getting your finger on the pulse of what is going on. Read a newspaper at least a few times a week.

Magazines marketed toward specific career groups are also great places to find information that you might not normally come into contact with. A magazine like *Psychology Today* might have articles dealing with the stress of dying. A story like this may heighten or assuage your fears about end of life issues and cause you to reconsider what you want spelled out in your advance directive, living will, or DNR order.

Read between the lines

While you are reading your newspapers, surfing the Internet, and flipping through magazines, be sure to remind yourself how this may affect you and where you live.

For example, some states have many provisions to help people handle POAs and other types of legal documents. If you live in one of these states, trends that are moving through the country may have a more immediate effect on your situation. If you live in a state that does not give specific legal information regarding POAs or other legal estate documents, national trends may not affect you as quickly or as directly.

It is important to be aware of your state's requirements regarding end-of-life issues so you can ensure you are making the best decisions for you and your family.

To Review:

Doing research can be intimidating and daunting, but a little direction can make researching POA topics much easier. When reading a book or magazine, highlight or otherwise mark information pertinent toy your situation. Using your tactile senses in addition to reading will help you retain information more completely. Make sure your research actually pertains to the information you need. While it is fine to ask your friends or close family members for advice, you should also personalize the information that you receive. Your situation may be similar to a situation they previously experienced, but there will be nuances unique to your situation. Finding information pertaining specifically to your situation will be more helpful than receiving advice from a friend who may send you in the wrong direction.

Chapter 11

Signing Your POA

Take it Seriously

The signing of a POA document is an important event. Indeed, it should be thought of with the same care and seriousness as a ritual, with key parties solemnly assembled and actions completed in proper order. You are entrusting your assets and, in some cases, your life to your attorney-in-fact. This is not an action to be taken lightly.

The POA Signing Ritual

How do you go about signing your completed POA document? Because you always need a notary and almost always need at least one witness (in addition to at least one notary; in some states, two), the signing is not simply a matter of putting pen to paper.

You are required to have at least one — often two — witnesses for the signing of your POA. These people do not need to have any legal expertise; they do not even need to know the contents of the document being signed. Their purpose is only to be there to witness the signing, and then to attest that they have done so by also signing the document. A witness must be a person not related to you or having an interest in the subject matter of the POA.

You will need to also enlist the services of a notary public. By and large, you can find one at a bank, but you may wish to do the signing at a notary's office or arrange to have the notary present wherever you plan to sign. Attorneys also have notaries at their offices and often are notaries themselves. Again, the notary is not expected to read or understand the particulars of the document. He or she is only providing official confirmation of your identity and that you have signed the document.

Witnesses and notaries also provide some protection against the possibility that a person might be forced to sign a POA against his or her wishes. With their presence at the signing, they can constitute a guard against coercion and fraud.

When everyone is assembled, you will sign the form where indicated, writing your name in exactly the same way it is typed on the form. If there are parts of the form that have been revised, crossed out, or amended, you will need to initial these parts in the margin. You will also initial any blanks that have been filled in with your choices. The signing and initialing should be done in black ink.

Once you have signed and initialed in all the necessary places, pass the document to the first witness, who will sign where indicated and then print his or her name. The second witness then does the same. Finally, the notary completes the notary's section of the form with a signature, stamp, and any other information required.

Some POA documents include a section for the attorney-in-fact and alternatives to write their signatures as well. This is to indicate their acceptance of the assigned role, although their signatures do not require witnessing or notarizing. It also serves as a "specimen" of the signature, against which the attorney-in-fact's later signature can be compared for verification.

After the document has been signed, make several copies of it. If a lawyer is setting up the POA, consider asking to have several originals made at the time of signing. One original is sufficient, though, as long as you keep it safe. The best place for a financial POA may be a safe-deposit box at the bank. For a health care POA, you may want to store it where others will be able to access it easily. This may not be a safe-deposit box. In this case, invest in a fireproof box or other indestructible container, and keep documents there. *Be sure to inform the attorney-in-fact, family members, and any other key people where you have put it.* In some jurisdictions, you will have the option of filing the POA as a public record. For some uses, this may be required.

If it is a health care POA, give copies of the document to family members, an attorney, a doctor, and the attorney-in-fact. If the document has anything to do with your material assets — if it is a financial POA — you will want your bank and other financial institutions (and also any creditors and vendors who may depend on the dictates of the document) to have a copy.

Have copies of the original POA certified by a notary public as true and accurate copies of the original document. For most uses of a POA, this certified copy will be acceptable to a third party.

Conclusion

Whether you decide to prepare your POA yourself or with the help of a trusted attorney, virtually anything you want to accomplish can be achieved if you plan in advance — but it is important to remain vigilant and see it through.

Knowing which POA form to use and choosing an attorney-in-fact can be a daunting task. There are not many laypeople who find legal documents easy to decipher. We hope that with the help of this book, you can now begin the process of determining your personal wishes. Further research will likely be needed to determine how your state handles POAs and other end-of-life documents. We hope this book served as a good primer to the subject and will make your quest for more information easier to understand.

By carefully planning your childcare, health care, and finan-cial POAs, you can accomplish all your goals and ensure your wishes are carried out in the event that you are unable to speak for yourself.

Preparing now for unplanned events is not only a smart decision — it is a decision your loved ones or business partners will be thankful for should the need arise to use your POA. Though thinking about the future and your possible incapacitation or death is stressful — and not a subject many of us prefer to dwell on — thinking through your wishes and how you would like your affairs to be managed can save those closest to you from further stress and emotional distraught.

The following appendices provide sample forms, charts, and other information you will find helpful. Remember: Many POA documents are state-specific. You may need to do further research to find the POA appropriate for your needs. The samples included in the appendices are only meant to familiarize you with the documents.

Appendix A

List of Power of Attorney Types

DOCUMENT TITLE	PURPOSE	NOTES
General Power of Attorney	Specifies certain areas of financial affairs to be managed by an attorney-in-fact.	Effective immediately. Invalid upon your divorce, death, revocation, or incapacity.
Unlimited Power of Attorney	Assigns all areas of your financial affairs to an attorney-in-fact.	Effective immediately. Invalid upon your divorce, death, revocation, or incapacity.
Limited Power of Attorney	Specifies certain areas of your financial affairs, or certain transactions or prevailing conditions, or certain periods in which an attorney-in-fact is authorized to represent you.	Invalid upon your divorce, death, revocation, or incapacity.
Power of Attorney for Real Estate	Designates a representative to act in your place for the purpose of transferring a particular piece of property.	Invalid upon your divorce, death, revocation, or incapacity.
Power of Attorney for Childcare	Designates a representative to act in your place as parent or guardian for the purpose of childcare, in temporary situations.	Invalid upon your divorce, death, revocation, or incapacity.
Durable Financial Power of Attorney	Assigns responsibilities for your financial affairs to an attorney-in-fact, to be effective either continuously (despite your incapacity), or to become effective (upon your incapacity).	Effective as specified in the document, and remains in effect until your revocation or death.
Durable Power of Attorney for Health Care	Names a chosen representative to serve as advocate for your interests in the event you become unable to make decisions due to medical reasons.	Effective upon your incapacity and remains in effect for the duration of your life, until your revocation, until you regain mental capacity, or until death.

When selecting the appropriate form for your needs, also pick up these ancillary documents, which may or may not come in handy:

- Affidavit of attorney-in-fact

- Revocation of POA

- Additional information for POA; a simple form that allows you more room for including special instructions as part of your official document

Appendix B

Sample POA and Estate Forms

If you have not worked with powers of attorney previously, the profusion of types and forms can be confusing. It is truly a fascinating study; individual state laws differ just as the 50 U.S. states (and let us not forget the District of Columbia) differ tremendously in their characters and traditions.

It is mostly a matter of literary style and formatting because the conferring of attorney-in-fact responsibilities itself requires only a few basic parameters to be set out. Nonetheless, legislators and attorneys find infinite ways to do this.

It is best to use the statutory forms provided by your state legislature. Check the chart on individual state laws to find your appropriate source.

In this appendix, we will examine samples of the various forms, so you can have some idea of what you are looking for when you start your process.

If you type in "power of attorney forms" on a search engine, you will get thousands of sources, and many of them advertise the availability of free forms. The free, printable forms tend to be minimalist and will likely need personalized additions or amendments. When you begin revising a POA, it is best to do so with an attorney so you avoid mistakes that could render your document useless. However, if you consult with an attorney, using free forms online will not even be necessary.

If you have special needs or circumstances to deal with, a Web site form might be a bit risky. But if you just want an extremely basic document, you can find a Web site to complete a state-specific form for you by answering their questionnaire completely.

Not all states have statutory forms for POAs as part of their legal code. This does not mean there are no specific requirements for the form. Often, the laws include exact verbiage, which is required to be used when an attorney creates the form. This is why, when you search for proper forms online, you do so by state, and the forms should conform to that state's specific specifications.

If your state does not supply forms, you will either work with a lawyer, or use forms obtained from the Internet or other sources.

Note that in the case of Financial POAs, particularly when using them for limited business or real estate, you may be required to use forms supplied by your bank, lending institution, or title insurance company.

Deciding which form to use is not simply a matter of personal taste. It cannot be overemphasized that you *need to check with your state laws first*. If you were to use one form without making sure it is compatible with legal requirements in your area, chances are good that you would not be signing, witnessing, or notarizing according to state guidelines. Neglecting these details renders the document invalid.

The law in your state may even spell out definitions of some controversial terms associated with health care POAs and other advance directives. Using these forms to ensure peace of mind regarding your care in old age is a relatively new practice. Anticipating misunderstandings, legislatures may endorse legal definitions of such terms as "permanently unconscious," "of sound mind," "incompetent," "comfort care," and even "health care." It is best to study these definitions if they exist in your state, so you will understand how decisions will be made about you.

Because state laws differ significantly, we will not attempt to look at all the existing variations of the many POA documents. Instead, what follows is a set of samples from random states. While any one of these samples may be typical, understand that none is universal.

Where to Find Blank Forms

As noted, it is perfectly possible and easy to fill in and complete your own POA form, especially if your situation is not overly complex. Given that life expectancy continues to increase, just about everyone should have a health care POA, and there is no need for a lawyer to oversee every one.

But you have also learned in this book that there are many variations of the forms. So, how do you know if the one you have will suffice?

Your local hospital will provide forms for health care POA and other advance directives. This is almost certainly the best place to get forms for this kind of power of attorney because they are obviously approved by the medical establishment with which you are likely to be dealing.

You can purchase generic forms at an office supply store. The cost will run between $5 and $30, depending on which package you buy. Read the specifics on the packaging to be sure it is the right form for you.

Online, your choices are immense. You can purchase blank forms and download them right away. Cost for blank forms is comparable to the in-store costs.

A couple of sites currently offer to deliver a form completely filled in and ready for your signature. After answering their questionnaire, submit the information and download the form.

- *Legal HelpMate* (**www.legalhelpmate.com/power-of-attorney.aspx**): Cost of filled-in form is around $25.

- *Standard Legal* (**www.standardlegal.com**): Here you can receive a downloaded, filled-in form for $30.

- *LawDepot.com* (**www.lawdepot.com/contracts/power-of-attorney-form**): This is a membership site, with a monthly fee required.

You may find this service offered on various attorneys' Web sites, as well.

When you are shopping online, be sure to purchase forms appropriate to your state. Most sites that offer these forms customize them to fit state requirements. If the site seems professional and up-to-date; the cost is not exorbitant; and the forms are state-specific, then this is an easy and relatively safe way to go.

As you investigate the many aspects of powers of attorney, you will most likely find yourself at the **www.FindLaw.com** site. This gigantic source of all things legal will not only lead you to the appropriate forms, but also will provide links to the legal code for your state. You can search by state or topic for information on any legal issue. The site also offers an attorney referral service.

The Web site of the Internet Legal Research Group (**www.ilrg. com**) offers free forms (which you will need to copy and paste to produce) or downloadable versions for just a few dollars. The site has links to state legal codes, law firm listings and ratings, complete forms and instructions for business legal needs, information for law students, a bookstore, and much more. Forms are compliant with state specifications, according to the organization; it even offers to pay $50 to anyone who can prove a discrepancy between the ILRG form and state law.

Finally, you can also go to your local bookstore, or to Amazon. com and purchase (for around $20 to $30) a book that contains blank documents, both in their generic form and as dictated by individual states. The book may also have a CD containing blank forms. Make sure that the forms offered are tailored to your state's requirements and that publication is relatively recent, at least within the past couple of years. State laws can change radically from year to year.

Following are some blank forms that you can use for reference:

General Power of Attorney

BY THIS DOCUMENT IT IS HEREBY ACKNOWLEDGED, that I, (name of person granting power of attorney) residing at (street address), (city), (state/province) (ZIP/postal code), the undersigned, do hereby appoint (name of person granted power of attorney) of (street address), (city), (state/province) (ZIP/postal code) as my attorney-in-fact ("Agent") to exercise the powers and discretions described below.

If the Agent is unable to serve for any reason, I appoint (alternative attorney-in-fact), of (street address), (city), (state/province) (ZIP/postal code), as my alternative or successory Agent, as the case may be to serve with the same powers and discretions.

I hereby revoke any and all general powers of attorney and special powers of attorney that previously have been signed by me. However, the preceding sentence shall not have the effect of revoking any powers of attorney that are directly related to my health care that previously have been signed by me.

My Agent shall have full power and authority to act on my behalf. This power and authority shall authorize my Agent to manage and conduct all of my affairs and to exercise all of my legal rights and powers, including all rights and powers that I may acquire in the future. My Agent's powers shall include, but not be limited to, the power to:

1. Open, maintain, or close bank accounts (including, but not limited to, checking accounts, savings accounts, and certificates of deposit), brokerage accounts, retirement plan accounts, and other similar accounts with financial institutions.

   a. Conduct any business with any banking or financial institution with respect to any of my accounts, including, but not limited to, making deposits and withdrawals; negotiating or endorsing any checks or other instruments with respect to any such accounts; and obtaining bank statements, passbooks, drafts, money orders, warrants, and certificates or vouchers payable to me by any person, firm, corporation or political entity.

   b. Perform any act necessary to deposit, negotiate, sell, or transfer any note, security, or draft of the United States of America, including U.S. Treasury Securities.

   c. Have access to any safe deposit box that I might own, including its contents.

2. Sell, exchange, buy, invest, or reinvest any assets or property owned by me. Such assets or property may include income-producing or non–income producing assets and property.

3. Take any and all legal steps necessary to collect any amount or debt owed to me, or to settle any claim, whether made against me or asserted on my behalf against any other person or entity.

4. Enter into binding contracts on my behalf.

5. Exercise all stock rights on my behalf as my proxy, including all rights with respect to stocks, bonds, debentures, commodities, options, or other investments.

6. Maintain and/or operate any business that I may own.

7. Employ professional and business assistance as may be appropriate, including attorneys, accountants, and real estate agents.

8. Sell, convey, lease, mortgage, manage, insure, improve, repair, or perform any other act with respect to any of my property (now owned or later acquired) including, but not limited to, real estate and real estate rights (including the right to remove tenants and to recover possession). This includes the right to sell or encumber any homestead that I now own or may own in the future.

9. Prepare, sign, and file documents with any governmental body or agency, including, but not limited to, authorization to:

    a. Prepare, sign, and file income and other tax returns with federal, state, local, and other governmental bodies.

    b. Obtain information or documents from any government or its agencies, and represent me in all tax matters, including the authority to negotiate, compromise, or settle any matter with such government or agency.

c. Prepare applications, provide information, and perform any other act reasonably requested by any government or its agencies in connection with governmental benefits (including medical, military, and social security benefits), and to appoint anyone, including my Agent, to act as my "Representative Payee" for the purpose of receiving Social Security benefits.

10. Make gifts from my assets to members of my family and to such other persons or charitable organizations with whom I have an established pattern of giving (or if it is appropriate to make such gifts for estate planning and/or tax purposes), to file state and federal gift tax returns, and to file a tax election to split gifts with my spouse, if any. No Agent acting under this instrument, except as specifically authorized in this instrument, shall have the power or authority to (a) gift, appoint, assign, or designate any of my assets, interests, or rights, directly or indirectly, to such Agent, such Agent's estate, such Agent's creditors, or the creditors of such Agent's estate, (b) exercise any powers of appointment I may hold in favor of such Agent, such Agent's estate, such Agent's creditors, or the creditors of such Agent's estate, or (c) use any of my assets to discharge any of such Agent's legal obligations, including any obligations of support, which such Agent may owe to others, *excluding* those whom I am legally obligated to support. For the purposes of making gifts to individuals under this provision, I appoint (name of gift agent), of (address), (city), (state/province) (ZIP/postal code), as my "Gift Agent." Provided that

they are not the same person, my Agent is authorized to make gifts, as appropriate, to my Gift Agent, and my Gift Agent is authorized to make gifts, as appropriate, to my Agent. Any gifts made to or for the benefit of my Agent or Gift Agent shall be limited to gifts that qualify for the federal gift tax annual exclusion, shall not exceed in value the federal gift tax annual exclusion amount in any one calendar year, and this annual right shall be non-cumulative and shall lapse at the end of each calendar year. If my Agent makes gifts to minors, such gifts may be made directly to the minor, to a parent, guardian, or next friend of the minor, or under the Uniform Gifts to Minors Act or the Uniform Transfers to Minors Act.

11. Transfer any of my assets to the trustee of any revocable trust created by me, if such trust is in existence at the time of such transfer.

12. Subject to other provisions of this document, disclaim any interest which might otherwise be transferred or distributed to me from any other person, estate, trust, or other entity, as may be appropriate. However, my Agent may not disclaim assets to which I would be entitled, if the result is that the disclaimed assets pass directly or indirectly to my Agent or my Agent's estate. Provided that they are not the same person, my Agent may disclaim assets that pass to my Gift Agent, and my Gift Agent may disclaim assets that pass to my Agent.

This Power of Attorney shall be construed broadly as a General Power of Attorney. The listing of specific powers is not intended to limit or restrict the general powers granted in this Power of Attorney in any manner.

Any power or authority granted to my Agent under this document shall be limited to the extent necessary to prevent this Power of Attorney from causing: (i) my income to be taxable to my Agent, (ii) my assets to be subject to a general power of appointment by my Agent, or (iii) my Agent to have any incidents of ownership with respect to any life insurance policies that I may own on the life of my Agent.

My Agent shall not be liable for any loss that results from a judgment error that was made in good faith. However, my Agent shall be liable for willful misconduct or the failure to act in good faith while acting under the authority of this Power of Attorney. A successor Agent shall not be liable for acts of a prior Agent.

No person who relies in good faith on the authority of my Agent under this instrument shall incur any liability to me, my estate, or my personal representative. I authorize my Agent to indemnify and hold harmless any third party who accepts and acts under this document.

If any part of any provision of this instrument shall be invalid or unenforceable under applicable law, such part shall be ineffective to the extent of such invalidity only, without in any way affecting the remaining parts of such provision or the remaining provisions of this instrument.

My Agent shall be entitled to reasonable compensation for any services provided as my Agent. My Agent shall be entitled to reimbursement of all reasonable expenses incurred as a result of carrying out any provision of this Power of Attorney.

My Agent shall provide an accounting for all funds handled and all acts performed as my Agent, but only if I so request or if such a request is made by any authorized personal representative or fiduciary acting on my behalf.

This Power of Attorney shall become effective immediately, and shall not be affected by my disability or lack of mental competence, except as may be provided otherwise by an applicable state statute. This is a Durable Power of Attorney. This Power of Attorney shall continue effective until my death. This Power of Attorney may be revoked by me at any time by providing written notice to my Agent.

Dated (month) (day), (year), at (city), (state).

_____

(Declarant's Name)

_____   _____

(Witness Signature)   (Witness Signature)

_____   _____

(Name)   (Name)

_____   _____

(City)   (City)

_____   _____

(State)   (State)

STATE OF _____

COUNTY OF _____

In _____, on the
_____ day of _____, 20____, before me, a Notary Public in and for the above state and county, personally appeared (**name of person granting power of attorney**), known to me or proved to be the person whose name is subscribed to the within instrument and acknowledged to me that he/she executed the same, and that by his/her signature on the instrument the person executed the instrument.

NOTARY PUBLIC_____

My Commission Expires _____
           (SEAL)

Revocation of Power of Attorney

I, (name of person revoking power of attorney - "principal"), of (city), (state), do hereby revoke the Power of Attorney dated (date power of attorney was authorized), and recorded (place and date power of attorney was recorded), that was granted to (name of person given power of attorney - "attorney-in-fact"), of (city), (state), and withdraw every power and authority conferred therein.

This instrument shall serve as notice to (attorney-in-fact) and to all interested persons that the above Power of Attorney hereby is null and void and of no further force or effect.

IN WITNESS WHEREOF, this instrument is executed under seal on

The _____ day of_____, _____.

Signed, sealed, and delivered in the presence of:

_____

North Carolina Statutory Short Form POA

This form is short in that it does not spell out the details of each area over which your attorney-in-fact has jurisdiction. The instructions include precise verbiage to add to the document if you wish to apply time limitations, or if you want it to be a durable POA. When adapting the form to be durable, be sure to check Article 2 of this Chapter in the North Carolina Statutes, where there are a number of special legal qualifications regarding durable powers.

Following the North Carolina form is a list of definitions for the areas your attorney-in-fact may influence in your interest. This is Chapter 32A-2 of the NC Statutes, entitled "Powers conferred by the Statutory Short Form Power of Attorney set out in G.S. 32A 1."

You will see that the list contains 15 items in North Carolina. There are 13 in Oklahoma; New York has 14; and in Wisconsin, 11 categories are listed. Clearly the states differ widely on the details they provide to clarify your understanding with your attorney-in-fact, so it is well-worth familiarizing yourself with your own laws and reading your document's fine print.

Powers of Attorney

Article 1.
Statutory Short Form Power of Attorney.

§ 32A 1. Statutory Short Form of General Power of Attorney. The use of the following form in the creation of a power of attorney is lawful, and, when used, it shall be construed in accordance with the provisions of this Chapter.

"NOTICE: THE POWERS GRANTED BY THIS DOCUMENT ARE BROAD AND SWEEPING. THEY ARE DEFINED IN CHAPTER 32A OF THE NORTH CAROLINA GENERAL STATUTES WHICH EXPRESSLY PERMITS THE USE OF ANY OTHER OR DIFFERENT FORM OF POWER OF ATTORNEY DESIRED BY THE PARTIES CONCERNED.

State of _____

County of _____

I_____, appoint_____
to be my attorney in fact, to act in my name in any way which
I could act for myself, with respect to the following matters as
each of them is defined in Chapter 32A of the North Carolina
General Statutes. *(DIRECTIONS: Initial the line opposite any one
or more of the subdivisions as to which the principal desires to give
the attorney in fact authority.)*

(1) Real property transactions _____

(2) Personal property transactions _____

(3) Bond, share, stock, securities, and
    commodity transactions _____

(4) Banking transactions _____

(5) Safe deposits _____

(6) Business operating transactions _____

(7) Insurance transactions _____

(8) Estate transactions _____

(9) Personal relationships and affairs _____

(10) Social security and unemployment _____

(11) Benefits from military service _____

(12) Tax matters _____

(13) Employment of agents _____

(14) Gifts to charities, and to individuals other than the attorney in fact _____

(15) Gifts to the named attorney in fact _____

(If power of substitution and revocation is to be given, add: 'I also give to such person full power to appoint another to act as my attorney in fact and full power to revoke such appointment.')

(If period of power of attorney is to be limited, add: 'This power terminates_____, _____')

(If power of attorney is to be a durable power of attorney under the provision of Article 2 of Chapter 32A and is to continue in effect after the incapacity or mental incompetence of the principal, add: 'This power of attorney shall not be affected by my subsequent incapacity or mental incompetence.')

(If power of attorney is to take effect only after the incapacity or mental incompetence of the principal, add: 'This power of attorney shall become effective after I become incapacitated or mentally incompetent.')

(If power of attorney is to be effective to terminate or direct the administration of a custodial trust created under the Uniform Custodial Trust Act, add: 'In the event of my subsequent incapacity or mental incompetence, the attorney in fact of this power of attorney shall have the power to terminate or to direct the administration of any custodial trust of which I am the beneficiary.')

(If power of attorney is to be effective to determine whether a beneficiary under the Uniform Custodial Trust Act is incapacitated or ceases to be incapacitated, add: 'The attorney in fact of this power of attorney shall have the power to determine whether I am incapacitated or whether my incapacity has ceased for the purposes of any custodial trust of which I am the beneficiary.')

Dated_____, _____ .

_____ (Seal)
                    (Signature)

STATE OF _____ COUNTY OF _____

On this_____ day of_____,_____,personally appeared before me, the said named _____ to me known and known to me to be the person described in and who executed the foregoing instrument and he (or she) acknowledged that he (or she) executed the same and being duly sworn by me, made oath that the statements in the foregoing instrument are true.

My Commission Expires _____.

_____
(Signature of Notary Public)
Notary Public (Official Seal)"

Oklahoma Statutory Form for Power of Attorney

Here is a General Financial POA, which may or may not be marked as durable, and it includes space for you to limit or extend the powers you are bestowing. Oklahoma requires notarization, but no witnesses are necessary to legally execute this document.

STATUTORY FORM FOR POWER OF ATTORNEY

A. The following statutory form of power of attorney is legally sufficient:

STATUTORY POWER OF ATTORNEY

NOTICE: THE POWERS GRANTED BY THIS DOCUMENT ARE BROAD AND SWEEPING. THEY ARE EXPLAINED IN THE UNIFORM STATUTORY FORM POWER OF ATTORNEY ACT. IF YOU HAVE ANY QUESTIONS ABOUT THESE POWERS, OBTAIN COMPETENT LEGAL ADVICE. THIS DOCUMENT DOES NOT AUTHORIZE ANYONE TO MAKE MEDICAL AND OTHER HEALTH CARE DECISIONS FOR YOU. YOU MAY REVOKE THIS POWER OF ATTORNEY IF YOU LATER WISH TO DO SO.

I _____ (insert your name and address) appoint _____ (insert the name and address of the person appointed) as my agent (attorney-in-fact) to act for me in any lawful way with respect to the following initialed subjects:

TO GRANT ALL OF THE FOLLOWING POWERS, INITIAL THE LINE IN FRONT OF (N) AND IGNORE THE LINES IN FRONT OF THE OTHER POWERS.

TO GRANT ONE OR MORE, BUT FEWER THAN ALL, OF THE FOLLOWING POWERS, INITIAL THE LINE IN FRONT OF EACH POWER YOU ARE GRANTING.

TO WITHHOLD A POWER, DO NOT INITIAL THE LINE IN FRONT OF IT. YOU MAY, BUT NEED NOT, CROSS OUT EACH POWER WITHHELD.

INITIAL

_____ (A) Real property transactions.

_____ (B) Tangible personal property transactions.

_____ (C) Stock and bond transactions.

_____ (D) Commodity and option transactions.

_____ (E) Banking and other financial institution transactions.

_____ (F) Business operating transactions.

_____ (G) Insurance and annuity transactions.

_____ (H) Estate, trust, and other beneficiary transactions.

_____ (I) Claims and litigation.

_____ (J) Personal and family maintenance.

_____ (K) Benefits from social security, Medicare, Medicaid, or other governmental programs or military service.

_____ (L) Retirement plan transactions.

_____ (M) Tax matters.

_____ (N) ALL OF THE POWERS LISTED ABOVE. YOU NEED NOT INITIAL ANY OTHER LINES IF YOU INITIAL LINE (N).

SPECIAL INSTRUCTIONS:

ON THE FOLLOWING LINES YOU MAY GIVE SPECIAL INSTRUCTIONS LIMITING OR EXTENDING THE POWERS GRANTED TO YOUR AGENT.

_____

_____

_____

_____

_____

_____

(Attach additional pages if needed.)

UNLESS YOU DIRECT OTHERWISE ABOVE, THIS POWER OF ATTORNEY IS EFFECTIVE IMMEDIATELY AND WILL CONTINUE UNTIL IT IS REVOKED.

This power of attorney will continue to be effective even though I become disabled, incapacitated, or incompetent.

STRIKE THE PRECEDING SENTENCE IF YOU DO NOT WANT THIS POWER OF ATTORNEY TO CONTINUE IF YOU BECOME DISABLED, INCAPACITATED, OR INCOMPETENT.

I agree that any third party who receives a copy of this document may act under it. Revocation of the power of attorney is not effective as to a third party until the third party learns of the revocation. I agree to indemnify the third party for any claims that arise against the third party because of reliance on this power of attorney.

Signed this _____ day of_____, 20 _____.

_____

(Your Signature)

_____

(Your Social Security Number)

State of _____

County of _____

This document was acknowledged before me on _____
(Date) by _____ (Name of Principal).

_____

(Signature of Notarial Officer)

_____

(Seal, If Any)

_____

(Title and Rank)

My commission expires: _____

BY ACCEPTING OR ACTING UNDER THE APPOINTMENT, THE AGENT ASSUMES THE FIDUCIARY AND OTHER LEGAL RESPONSIBILITIES OF AN AGENT.

B. A statutory power of attorney is legally sufficient under this act, if the wording of the form complies substantially with subsection A of this section, the form is properly completed, and the signature of the principal is acknowledged.

C. If the line in front of (N) of the form under subsection A of this section is initialed, an initial on the line in front of any other power does not limit the powers granted by line (N).

Historical Data

Added by Laws 1998, c. 420, § 3, eff. Nov. 1, 1998.

Durable General Power of Attorney Effective at a Future Time (New York Springing POA)

The example shows a statutory springing power of attorney, the form adapted to become effective at a specified time in the future, which is frequently when a certain event occurs or the principal is declared incapacitated. Notice the large number of agents allowed by this form. New York is rare in its statutory inclusion of this particular POA form. Much more often, a financial POA's durability or non-durability will be specified within the basic form.

DURABLE GENERAL POWER OF ATTORNEY EFFECTIVE
AT A FUTURE TIME
NEW YORK STATUTORY SHORT FORM

(CAUTION: THIS IS AN IMPORTANT DOCUMENT. IT GIVES THE PERSON WHOM YOU DESIGNATE (YOUR "AGENT") BROAD POWERS TO HANDLE YOUR PROPERTY DURING YOUR LIFETIME, WHICH MAY INCLUDE POWERS TO MORTGAGE, SELL, OR OTHERWISE DISPOSE OF ANY REAL OR PERSONAL PROPERTY WITHOUT ADVANCE NOTICE TO YOU OR APPROVAL BY YOU. THESE POWERS MAY ONLY BE USED AFTER A CERTIFICATION THAT YOU HAVE BECOME DISABLED, INCAPACITATED, OR INCOMPETENT, OR THAT SOME OTHER EVENT HAS OCCURRED. THESE POWERS ARE EXPLAINED MORE FULLY IN NEW YORK GENERAL OBLIGATIONS LAW, ARTICLE 5, TITLE 15, SECTIONS 5-1502A THROUGH 5-1506, WHICH EXPRESSLY PERMITS THE USE OF ANY OTHER OR DIFFERENT FORM OF POWER OF ATTORNEY.

THIS DOCUMENT DOES NOT AUTHORIZE ANYONE TO MAKE MEDICAL OR OTHER HEALTH CARE DECISIONS. YOU MAY EXECUTE A HEALTH CARE PROXY TO DO THIS.

IF THERE IS ANYTHING ABOUT THIS FORM THAT YOU DO NOT UNDERSTAND, YOU SHOULD ASK A LAWYER TO EXPLAIN IT TO YOU.)

THIS is intended to constitute a POWER OF ATTORNEY EFFECTIVE AT A FUTURE TIME pursuant to Article 5, Title 15 of the New York General Obligations Law:

I, _____

(Insert your name and address)

do hereby appoint: _____

(If 1 person is to be appointed agent, insert the name and address of your agent above)

_____

_____

_____

_____

(If 2 or more persons are to be appointed agents by you, insert their names and addresses above)

my attorney(s)-in-fact TO ACT (If more than one agent is designated, CHOOSE ONE of the following two choices by putting your initials in ONE of the blank spaces ( ) to the left of your choice:)

   ( ) Each agent may SEPARATELY act.
   ( ) All agents must act TOGETHER.

(If neither blank space is initialed, the agents will be required to act TOGETHER)

TO TAKE EFFECT upon the occasion of the signing of a written statement EITHER:

(INSTRUCTIONS: COMPLETE OR OMIT SECTION (I) —OR— SECTION (II) BELOW BUT NEVER COMPLETE BOTH SECTIONS (I) AND (II) BELOW. IF YOU DO NOT COMPLETE EITHER SECTION (I) OR SECTION (II) BELOW,

IT SHALL BE PRESUMED THAT YOU WANT THE PROVISIONS OF SECTION (I) BELOW TO APPLY)

(I) by a physician or physicians named herein by me at this point:

Dr. _____

_____

(insert full name(s) and address(es) of certifying physician(s) chosen by you)

or if no physician or physicians are named hereinabove, or if the physician or physicians named hereinabove are unable to act, by my regular physician, or by a physician who has treated me within one year preceding the date of such signing, or by a licensed psychologist or psychiatrist, certifying that I am suffering from diminished capacity that would preclude me from conducting my affairs in a competent manner;

—OR—

(II) by a person or persons named herein by me at this point:

_____

_____

(insert full name(s) and address(es) of certifying physician(s) chosen by you)

CERTIFYING that the following specified event has occurred:

_____

_____

(insert hereinabove the specified event the certification of which will cause THIS POWER OF ATTORNEY to take effect)

IN MY NAME, PLACE, AND STEAD in any way which I myself could do, if I were personally present, with respect to the following matters as each of them is defined in Title 15 of Article 5 of the New York General Obligations Law to the extent that I am permitted by law to act through an agent:

(DIRECTIONS: Initial in the blank space to the left of your choice any one or more of the following lettered subdivisions as to which you WANT to give your agent authority. If the blank space to the left of any particular lettered subdivision is NOT initialed, NO AUTHORITY WILL BE GRANTED for matters that are included in that subdivision. Alternatively, the letter corresponding to each power you wish to grant may be written or typed on the blank line in subdivision "(Q)", and you may then put your initials in the blank space to the left of subdivision "(Q)" in order to grant each of the powers so indicated)

( ) (A) real estate transactions;

( ) (B) chattel and goods transactions;

( ) (C) bond, share and commodity transactions;

( ) (D) banking transactions;

( ) (E) business operating transactions;

( ) (F) insurance transactions;

( ) (G) estate transactions;

( ) (H) claims and litigation;

( ) (I) personal relationships and affairs;

( ) (J) benefits from military service;

( ) (K) records, reports and statements;

( ) (L) retirement benefit transactions;

( ) (M) making gifts to my spouse, children and more remote descendants, and parents, not to exceed in the ag-
gregate $10,000 to each of such persons in any year;

( ) (N) tax matters;

( ) (O) all other matters;

( ) (P) full and unqualified authority to my attorney(s)-
in-fact to delegate any or all of the foregoing powers
to any person or persons whom my attorney(s)-in-fact
shall select;

( ) (Q) each of the above matters identified by the following letters:

_____

This durable Power of Attorney shall not be affected by my
subsequent disability or incompetence.

(Special provisions and limitations may be included in the
statutory short form power of attorney effective at a future
time only if they conform to the requirements of section 5-1503
of the New York General Obligations Law.)

_____

_____

_____

If every agent named above is unable or unwilling to serve, I
appoint _____ (insert name and address
of successor) to be my agent for all purposes hereunder.

TO INDUCE ANY THIRD PARTY TO ACT HEREUNDER, I HEREBY AGREE THAT ANY THIRD PARTY RECEIVING A DULY EXECUTED COPY OR FACSIMILE OF THIS INSTRUMENT TOGETHER WITH A DULY EXECUTED COPY OR FACSIMILE OF THE WRITTEN STATEMENT OR STATEMENTS OF CERTIFICATION REQUIRED FOR THIS INSTRUMENT TO BE EFFECTIVE MAY ACT HEREUNDER, AND THAT THE SUSPENSION, REVOCATION OR TERMINATION HEREOF SHALL BE INEFFECTIVE AS TO SUCH THIRD PARTY UNLESS AND UNTIL ACTUAL NOTICE OR KNOWLEDGE OF SUCH SUSPENSION, REVOCATION OR TERMINATION SHALL HAVE BEEN RECEIVED BY SUCH THIRD PARTY, AND I FOR MYSELF AND FOR MY HEIRS, EXECUTORS, LEGAL REPRESENTATIVES AND ASSIGNS, HEREBY AGREE TO INDEMNIFY AND HOLD HARMLESS ANY SUCH THIRD PARTY FROM AND AGAINST ANY AND ALL CLAIMS THAT MAY ARISE AGAINST SUCH THIRD PARTY BY REASON OF SUCH THIRD PARTY HAVING RELIED ON THE PROVISIONS OF THIS INSTRUMENT.

THIS GENERAL POWER OF ATTORNEY EFFECTIVE AT A FUTURE TIME MAY BE REVOKED BY ME AT ANY TIME.

In Witness Whereof I have hereunto signed my name this _____ day of _____, 20 _____ .

(YOU SIGN HERE:) _____
(Signature of Principal)

Advance Health Care Directive Form

(CALIFORNIA PROBATE CODE SECTION 4700-4701)

4700. The form provided in Section 4701 may, but need not, be used to create an advance health care directive. The other sections of this division govern the effect of the form or any other writing used to create an advance health care directive. An individual may complete or modify all or any part of the form in Section 4701.

4701. The statutory advance health care directive form is as follows:

ADVANCE HEALTH CARE DIRECTIVE
(California Probate Code Section 4701)

Explanation
You have the right to give instructions about your own health care. You also have the right to name someone else to make health care decisions for you. This form lets you do either or both of these things. It also lets you express your wishes regarding donation of organs and the designation of your primary physician. If you use this form, you may complete or modify all or any part of it. You are free to use a different form.

Part 1 of this form is a power of attorney for health care. Part 1 lets you name another individual as agent to make health care decisions for you if you become incapable of making your own decisions or if you want someone else to make those decisions for you now even though you are still capable. You may also name an alternative agent to act for you if your first choice is not willing, able, or reasonably available to make decisions for you. (Your agent may not be an operator or employee of a community care facility or a residential care facility where you are receiving care, or your supervising health care provider or employee of the health care institution where you are receiving care, unless your agent is related to you or is a coworker.)

Unless the form you sign limits the authority of your agent, your agent may make all health care decisions for you. This form has a place for you to limit the authority of your agent. You need not limit the authority of your agent if you wish to rely on your agent for all health care decisions that may have to be made. If you choose not to limit the authority of your agent, your agent will have the right to:

(a) Consent or refuse consent to any care, treatment, service, or procedure to maintain, diagnose, or otherwise affect a physical or mental condition.

(b) Select or discharge health care providers and institutions.

(c) Approve or disapprove diagnostic tests, surgical procedures, and programs of medication.

(d) Direct the provision, withholding, or withdrawal of artificial nutrition and hydration and all other forms of health care, including cardiopulmonary resuscitation.

(e) Make anatomical gifts, authorize an autopsy, and direct disposition of remains.

Part 2 of this form lets you give specific instructions about any aspect of your health care, whether or not you appoint an agent.

Choices are provided for you to express your wishes regarding the provision, withholding, or withdrawal of treatment to keep you alive, as well as the provision of pain relief. Space is also provided for you to add to the choices you have made or for you to write out any additional wishes. If you are satisfied to allow your agent to determine what is best for you in making end-of-life decisions, you need not fill out Part 2 of this form.

Part 3 of this form lets you express an intention to donate your bodily organs and tissues following your death.

Part 4 of this form lets you designate a physician to have primary responsibility for your health care.

After completing this form, sign and date the form at the end.

The form must be signed by two qualified witnesses or acknowledged before a notary public. Give a copy of the signed and completed form to your physician, to any other health care providers you may have, to any health care institution at which you are receiving care, and to any health care agents you have named. You should talk to the person you have named as agent to make sure that he or she understands your wishes and is willing to take the responsibility.

You have the right to revoke this advance health care directive or replace this form at any time.

Power of Attorney for Health Care

PART 1

(1.1) DESIGNATION OF AGENT: I designate the following individual as my agent to make health care decisions for me:

_____

(Name of Individual)

_____

(Address) (City) (State) (ZIP Code)

_____

(Home Phone) (Work Phone)

OPTIONAL: If I revoke my agent's authority or if my agent is not willing, able, or reasonably available to make a health care decision for me, I designate as my first alternative agent:

_____

(Name of Individual)

_____

(Address) (City) (State) (ZIP Code)

_____

(Home Phone) (Work Phone)

(1.2) AGENT'S AUTHORITY: My agent is authorized to make all health care decisions for me, including decisions to provide, withhold, or withdraw artificial nutrition and hydration and all other forms of health care to keep me alive, except as I state here:

_____

_____

(Add additional sheets if needed.)

(1.3) WHEN AGENT'S AUTHORITY BECOMES EFFEC-TIVE: My agent's authority becomes effective when my primary physician determines that I am unable to make my own health care decisions unless I mark the following box.

If I mark this box ( ), my agent's authority to make health care decisions for me takes effect immediately.

(1.4) AGENT'S OBLIGATION: My agent shall make health care decisions for me in accordance with this power of attorney for health care, any instructions I give in Part 2 of this form, and my other wishes to the extent known to my agent. To the extent my wishes are unknown, my agent shall make health care decisions for me in accordance with what my agent determines to be in my best interest. In determining my best interest, my agent shall consider my personal values to the extent known to my agent.

(1.5) AGENT'S POSTDEATH AUTHORITY: My agent is authorized to make anatomical gifts, authorize an autopsy, and direct disposition of my remains, except as I state here or in Part 3 of this form:

_____

_____

(Add additional sheets if needed.)

(1.6) NOMINATION OF CONSERVATOR: If a conservator of my person needs to be appointed for me by a court, I nominate the agent designated in this form. If that agent is not willing, able, or reasonably available to act as conservator, I nominate the alternative agents whom I have named, in the order designated.

PART 2
INSTRUCTIONS FOR HEALTH CARE

If you fill out this part of the form, you may strike any wording you do not want.

(2.1) END-OF-LIFE DECISIONS: I direct that my health care providers and others involved in my care provide, withhold, or withdraw treatment in accordance with the choice I have marked below:

☐ **(a)** **Choice Not To Prolong Life.** I do not want my life to be prolonged if (1) I have an incurable and irreversible condition that will result in my death within a relatively short time, (2) I become unconscious and, to a reasonable degree of medical certainty, I will not regain consciousness, or (3) the likely risks and burdens of treatment would outweigh the expected benefits,

OR

☐ **(b)** **Choice To Prolong Life.** I want my life to be prolonged as long as possible within the limits of generally accepted health care standards.

(2.2) RELIEF FROM PAIN: Except as I state in the following space, I direct that treatment for alleviation of pain or discomfort be provided at all times, even if it hastens my death:

_____

_____

(Add additional sheets if needed.)

(2.3) OTHER WISHES: (If you do not agree with any of the optional choices above and wish to write your own, or if you wish to add to the instructions you have given above, you may do so here.)

I direct that:

_____

_____

_____

_____

_____

(Add additional sheets if needed.)

PART 3
DONATION OF ORGANS AT DEATH
(OPTIONAL)

(3.1) Upon my death (mark applicable box):

☐ (a) I give any needed organs, tissues, or parts, OR

☐ (b) I give the following organs, tissues, or parts only.

_____

(c) My gift is for the following purposes (strike any of the following you do not want):

(1) Transplant
(2) Therapy
(3) Research
(4) Education

PART 4
PRIMARY PHYSICIAN
(OPTIONAL)

(4.1) I designate the following physician as my primary physician:

_____

(Name of Physician)

_____

(Address) (City) (State) (ZIP Code)

_____

(Phone)

OPTIONAL: If the physician I have designated above is not willing, able, or reasonably available to act as my primary physician, I designate the following physician as my primary physician:

_____

(Name of Physician)

_____

(Address) (City) (State) (ZIP Code)

_____

(Phone)

PART 5

(5.1) EFFECT OF COPY: A copy of this form has the same effect as the original.

(5.2) SIGNATURE: Sign and date the form here:

_____   _____
(Date)   (Sign Your Name)

_____   _____
(Address)   (Print Your Name)

_____   _____
(City)   (State)

(5.3) STATEMENT OF WITNESSES: I declare under penalty of perjury under the laws of California (1) that the individual who signed or acknowledged this advance health care directive is personally known to me, or that the individual's identity was proved to me by convincing evidence, (2) that the individual signed or acknowledged this advance directive in my presence, (3) that the individual appears to be of sound mind and under no duress, fraud, or undue influence, (4) that I am not a person appointed as agent by this advance directive, and (5) that I am not the individual's health care provider, an employee of the individual's health care provider, the operator of a community care facility, an employee of an operator of a of a community care facility, the operator of a residential care facility for the elderly, nor an employee of an operator of a residential care facility for the elderly.

_____   _____
(First Witness)   (Second Witness)

_____   _____
(Print Name)   (Print Name)

_____   _____
(Address)   (Address)

(City) (State)	(City) (State)
(Signature of Witness)	(Signature of Witness)
(Date)	(Date)

(5.4) ADDITIONAL STATEMENT OF WITNESSES: At least one of the above witnesses must also sign the following declaration:

I further declare under penalty of perjury under the laws of California that I am not related to the individual executing this advance health care directive by blood, marriage, or adoption, and to the best of my knowledge, I am not entitled to any part of the individual's estate upon his or her death under a will now existing or by operation of law.

_____   _____
(Signature of Witness)   (Signature of Witness)

PART 6
SPECIAL WITNESS REQUIREMENT

(6.1) The following statement is required only if you are a patient in a skilled nursing facility — a health care facility that provides the following basic services: skilled nursing care and supportive care to patients whose primary need is for availability of skilled nursing care on an extended basis. The patient advocate or ombudsman must sign the following statement:

STATEMENT OF PATIENT ADVOCATE OR OMBUDSMAN

I declare under penalty of perjury under the laws of California that I am a patient advocate or ombudsman as designated by the State Department of Aging and that I am serving as a witness as required by Section 4675 of the Probate Code.

_____   _____
(Date)   (Sign Your Name)

_____   _____
(Address)   (Print Your Name)

_____   _____
(City)   (State)

October 2006

Illinois Living Will Act (755 ILCS 35)

Under this statute, a person who has a terminal condition has the right to sign a "written declaration instructing his or her physician to withhold or withdraw death delaying procedures." A terminal condition is defined as "an incurable and irreversible condition which is such that death is imminent and the application of death-delaying procedures serves only to prolong the dying process."

A person age 18 who is of sound mind may execute a living will or direct someone to sign it for him in his presence and also in the presence of two witnesses age at least 18. The living will is then provided to the treating physician and other pertinent medical providers. It should also be given to family members to make them aware of your wishes.

The statute suggests the following as a form that may be used to express a written living will:

DECLARATION

This declaration is made this _____ day of _____ (month, year). I, _____, being of sound mind, willfully and voluntarily make known my desires that my moment of death shall not be artificially postponed.

If at any time I should have an incurable and irreversible injury, disease, or illness judged to be a terminal condition by my attending physician who has personally examined me and has determined that my death is imminent except for death delaying procedures, I direct that such procedures which would only prolong the dying process be withheld or withdrawn, and that I be permitted to die naturally with only the administration of medication, sustenance, or the performance of any medical procedure deemed necessary by my attending physician to provide me with comfort care.

In the absence of my ability to give directions regarding the use of such death delaying procedures, it is my intention that this declaration shall be honored by my family and physician as the final expression of my legal right to refuse medical or surgical treatment and accept the consequences from such refusal.

Signed _____

City, County, and State of Residence _____

The declarant is personally known to me and I believe him or her to be of sound mind. I saw the declarant sign the declaration in my presence (or the declarant acknowledged in my presence that he or she had signed the declaration) and I signed the declaration as a witness in the presence of the declarant. I did not sign the declarant's signature above for or at the direction of the declarant. At the date of this instrument, I am not entitled to any portion of the estate of the declarant according to the laws of intestate succession or, to the best of my knowledge and belief, under any will of declarant or other instrument taking effect at declarant's death, or directly financially responsible for declarant's medical care.

Witness _____

Witness _____

Illinois Health Care Surrogate Act (755 ILCS 40)

This Act recognizes that the right to forego life sustaining treatment should not be pre-empted by a lack of decisional capacity caused by a person's illness or condition. Under this law, Illinois provides for appointment of another person to make the decision, i.e., a surrogate. The authority to act vested under this statute steps in where there is not already on record a Living Will. A surrogate decisionmaker means "an adult individual or individuals who (i) have decisional capacity, (ii) are available upon reasonable inquiry, (iii) are willing to make medical treatment decisions on behalf of a patient who lacks decisional capacity, and (iv) are identified by the attending physician in accordance with the provisions of this Act as the person or persons who are to make those decisions in accordance with the provisions of this Act."

Illinois Power of Attorney Act (755 ILCS 45)

A durable power of attorney is another means of appointing someone to act in your behalf should you become incapacitate physically and/or mentally. This document can conceivably incorporate living will wishes and also eliminate the necessity of the need for appointment of a surrogate on your behalf. This is a document you want to prepare with assistance of an Illinois attorney. The ideal recommendation is to execute a durable power of attorney and also a living will, making sure the documents are in accord with each other. The power of attorney is a broader document than a living will.

Indiana Living Will Declaration

(Statutory Form, IC 15-35-4-10)

Declaration made this _____ day of _____ (month, year). I, _____, being at least eighteen (18) years of age and of sound mind, willfully and voluntarily make known my desires that my dying shall not be artificially prolonged under the circumstances set forth below, and I declare:

If at any time my attending physician certifies in writing that: (1) I have an incurable injury, disease, or illness; (2) my death will occur within a short time; and (3) the use of life-prolonging procedures would serve only to artificially prolong the dying process, I direct that such procedures be withheld or withdrawn, and that I be permitted to die naturally with only the performance or provision of any medical procedure or medication necessary to provide me with comfort care or to alleviate pain, and, if I have so indicated below, the provision of artificially supplied nutrition and hydration. (Indicate your choice by initialing or making your mark before signing this declaration):

_____ I wish to receive artificially supplied nutrition and hydration, even if the effort to sustain life is futile or excessively burdensome to me.

_____ I do not wish to receive artificially supplied nutrition and hydration, if the effort to sustain life is futile or excessively burdensome to me.

_____ I intentionally make no decision concerning artificially supplied nutrition and hydration, leaving the decision to my health care representative appointed under IC 16-36-1-7 or my attorney in fact with health care powers under IC 30-5-5.'

In the absence of my ability to give directions regarding the use of life prolonging procedures, it is my intention that this declaration be honored by my family and physician as the final expression of my legal right to refuse medical or surgical treatment and accept the consequences of the refusal.

I understand the full import of this declaration.

Signed _____

_____
(City, County, and State of Residence)

The declarant has been personally known to me, and I believe (him/her) to be of sound mind. I did not sign the declarant's signature above for or at the direction of the declarant. I am not a parent, spouse, or child of the declarant. I am not entitled to any part of the declarant's estate or directly financially responsible for the declarant's medical care. I am competent and at least eighteen (18) years of age.

_____   _____
Witness   Date

_____   _____
Witness   Date

Note that the living will must be voluntarily written by a person at least 18 years of age, signed and witnessed by two persons who are close relatives or entitled to inherit from the estate of the declarant at death. It is important to note that Indiana law does not allow enforcement of a Living Will during the time a declarant is pregnant.

Indiana Life-Prolonging Procedures Declaration

(Statutory Form, IC 15-35-4-11)

Declaration made this _____ day of _____ (month, year). I, _____, being at least eighteen (18) years of age and of sound mind, willfully and voluntarily make known my desire that if at any time I have an incurable injury, disease, or illness determined to be a terminal condition I request the use of life prolonging procedures that would extend my life. This includes appropriate nutrition and hydration, the administration of medication, and the performance of all other medical procedures necessary to extend my life, to provide comfort care, or to alleviate pain.

In the absence of my ability to give directions regarding the use of life prolonging procedures, it is my intention that this declaration be honored by my family and physician as the final expression of my legal right to request medical or surgical treatment and accept the consequences of the request.

I understand the full import of this declaration.

Signed _____

_____
(City, County, and State of Residence)

The declarant has been personally known to me, and I believe (him/her) to be of sound mind. I am competent and at least eighteen (18) years of age.

_____   _____
(Witness)   (Date)

_____   _____
(Witness)   (Date)

Statutory Living Will Form in North Carolina

ADVANCE DIRECTIVE FOR A NATURAL DEATH ("LIVING WILL")

NOTE: YOU SHOULD USE THIS DOCUMENT TO GIVE YOUR HEALTH CARE PROVIDERS INSTRUCTIONS TO WITHHOLD OR WITHDRAW LIFE-PROLONGING

MEASURES IN CERTAIN SITUATIONS. THERE IS NO LEGAL REQUIREMENT THAT ANYONE EXECUTE A LIVING WILL.

GENERAL INSTRUCTIONS: You can use this Advance Directive ("Living Will") form to give instructions for the future if you want your health care providers to withhold or withdraw life prolonging measures in certain situations. You should talk to your doctor about what these terms mean. The Living Will states what choices you would have made for yourself if you were able to communicate. Talk to your family members, friends, and others you trust about your choices. Also, it is a good idea to talk with professionals such as your doctors, clergypersons, and lawyers before you complete and sign this Living Will.

You do not have to use this form to give those instructions, but if you create your own Advance Directive you need to be very careful to ensure that it is consistent with North Carolina law.

This Living Will form is intended to be valid in any jurisdiction in which it is presented, but places outside North Carolina may impose requirements that this form does not meet.

*If you want to use this form, you must complete it, sign it, and have your signature witnessed by two qualified witnesses and proved by a notary public. Follow the instructions about which choices you can initial very carefully. **Do not sign this form until** two witnesses and a notary public are present to watch you sign it. You then should consider giving a copy to your primary physician and/ or a trusted relative, and should consider filing it with the Advanced Health Care Directive Registry maintained by the North Carolina Secretary of State: **www.nclifelinks.org/ahcdr**.*

My Desire for a Natural Death

I, _____, being of sound mind, desire that, as specified below, my life not be prolonged by life-prolonging measures:

1. When My Directives Apply

My directions about prolonging my life shall apply *IF* my attending physician determines that I lack capacity to make or communicate health care decisions and:

NOTE: YOU MAY INITIAL ANY AND ALL OF THESE CHOICES.

_____
(Initial)   I have an incurable or irreversible condition that will result in my death within a relatively short period of time.

_____
(Initial)   I become unconscious and my health care providers determine that, to a high degree of medical certainty, I will never regain my consciousness.

_____
(Initial)   I suffer from advanced dementia or any other condition which results in the substantial loss of my cognitive ability and my health care providers determine that, to a high degree of medical certainty, this loss is not reversible.

2. These are My Directives about Prolonging My Life:

In those situations I have initialed in Section 1, I direct that my health care providers:

NOTE: INITIAL ONLY IN ONE PLACE.

_____ may withhold or withdraw life prolonging
(Initial)   measures.

_____ shall withhold or withdraw life prolonging
(Initial)   measures.

3. Exceptions – "Artificial Nutrition or Hydration"

NOTE: INITIAL ONLY IF YOU WANT TO MAKE EXCEPTIONS TO YOUR INSTRUCTIONS IN PARAGRAPH 2.

EVEN THOUGH I do not want my life prolonged in those situations I have initialed in Section 1:

_____ I *DO* want to receive BOTH artificial hydration *and*
(Initial)   artificial nutrition (for example, through tubes) in those situations.

NOTE: DO NOT INITIAL THIS BLOCK IF ONE OF THE BLOCKS BELOW IS INITIALED.

_____ I *DO* want to receive ONLY artificial hydration (for
(Initial)   example, through tubes) in those situations.

NOTE: DO NOT INITIAL THE BLOCK ABOVE OR BELOW IF THIS BLOCK IS INITIALED.

_____ I DO want to receive ONLY artificial nutrition (for
(Initial)   example, through tubes) in those situations.

NOTE: DO NOT INITIAL EITHER OF THE TWO BLOCKS ABOVE IF THIS BLOCK IS INITIALED.

4. I Wish to be Made as Comfortable as Possible

I direct that my health care providers take reasonable steps to keep me as clean, comfortable, and free of pain as possible so that my dignity is maintained, even though this care may hasten my death.

5. I Understand my Advance Directive

I am aware and understand that this document directs certain life-prolonging measures to be withheld or discontinued in accordance with my advance instructions.

6. If I have an Available Health Care Agent

If I have appointed a health care agent by executing a health care power of attorney or similar instrument, and that health care agent is acting and available and gives instructions that differ from this Advance Directive, then I direct that:

_____
(Initial)   Follow Advance Directive: This Advance Directive will **override** instructions my health care agent gives about prolonging my life.

_____
(Initial)   Follow Health Care Agent: My health care agent has authority to override this Advance Directive.

NOTE: DO NOT INITIAL BOTH BLOCKS. *IF YOU DO NOT INITIAL EITHER BOX, THEN YOUR HEALTH CARE PROVIDERS WILL FOLLOW THIS ADVANCE DIRECTIVE AND IGNORE THE INSTRUCTIONS OF YOUR HEALTH CARE AGENT ABOUT PROLONGING YOUR LIFE.*

7. **My Health Care Providers May Rely on this Directive**

   My health care providers shall not be liable to me or to my family, my estate, my heirs, or my personal representative for following the instructions I give in this instrument. Following my directions shall not be considered suicide, or the cause of my death, or malpractice, or unprofessional conduct. If I have revoked this instrument but my health care providers do not know that I have done so, and they follow the instructions in this instrument in good faith, they shall be entitled to the same protections to which they would have been entitled if the instrument had not been revoked.

8. **I Want this Directive to be Effective Anywhere**

   I intend that this Advance Directive be followed by any health care provider in any place.

9. **I have the Right to Revoke this Advance Directive**

   I understand that at any time I may revoke this Advance Directive in a writing I sign, or by communicating in any clear and consistent manner my intent to revoke it to my attending physician. I understand that if I revoke this instrument, I should try to destroy all copies of it.

This the _____ day of _____, _____.

_____
(Print Name)

I hereby state that the declarant, _____,
being of sound mind, signed (or directed another to sign on
declarant's behalf) the foregoing Advance Directive for a Natural Death in my presence, and that I am not related to the
declarant by blood or marriage, and I would not be entitled to
any portion of the estate of the declarant under any existing
will or codicil of the declarant or as an heir under the Intestate
Succession Act, if the declarant died on this date without a
will. I also state that I am not the declarant's attending physician, nor a licensed health care provider who is (1) an employee of the declarant's attending physician, (2) nor an employee
of the health facility in which the declarant is a patient, or (3)
an employee of a nursing home or any adult care home where
the declarant resides. I further state that I do not have any
claim against the declarant or the estate of the declarant.

Date: _____

Witness: _____

Date: _____

Witness: _____

_____COUNTY, _____STATE

Sworn to (or affirmed) and subscribed before me this day by

_____

_____
(Type/Print Name of Declarant)

_____
(Type/Print Name of Witness)

_____
(Type/Print Name of Witness)

Date: _____

_____   _____
(Official Seal)   (Signature of Notary Public)

_____, Notary Public
(Printed or Typed Name)

My commission expires: _____

Pennsylvania Advance Health Care Declaration Statutory Form

(Statute 20-§5404)

I, _____, being of sound mind, willfully and voluntarily make this declaration to be followed if I become incompetent. This declaration reflects my firm and settled commitment to refuse life-sustaining treatment under the circumstances indicated below.

I direct my attending physician to withhold or withdraw life-sustaining treatment that serves only to prolong the process of my dying, if I should be in a terminal condition or in a state of permanent unconsciousness.

I direct that treatment be limited to measures to keep me comfortable and to relieve pain, including any pain that might occur by withholding or withdrawing life-sustaining treatment.

In addition, if I am in the condition described above, I feel especially strong about the following forms of treatment:

I ☐ do ☐ do not want cardiac resuscitation.

I ☐ do ☐ do not want mechanical respiration.

I ☐ do ☐ do not want tube feeding or any other artificial or invasive form of nutrition (food) or hydration (water).

I ☐ do ☐ do not want blood or blood products.

I ☐ do ☐ do not want any form of surgery or invasive diagnostic tests.

I □ do □ do not want kidney dialysis.

I □ do □ do not want antibiotics.

I realize that if I do not specifically indicate my preference regarding any of the forms of treatment listed above, I may receive that form of treatment.

Other instructions:

I □ do □ do not want to designate another person as my surrogate to make medical treatment decisions for me if I should be incompetent and in a terminal condition or in a state of permanent unconsciousness.

Name and address of surrogate (if applicable): _____

_____

Name and address of substitute surrogate (if surrogate designated above is unable to serve): _____

_____

I □ do □ do not want to make an anatomical gift of all or part of my body, subject to the following limitations, if any:

_____

_____

I made this declaration on the _____ day of (month, year).

Declarant's signature: _____

Declarant's address: _____

The declarant or the person on behalf of and at the direction of the declarant knowingly and voluntarily signed this writing by signature or mark in my presence.

Witness's signature: _____

Witness's address: _____

Witness's signature: _____

Witness's address: _____

This Declaration becomes operative under Pennsylvania law when a copy of it is given to your attending physician and your physician determines you "to be incompetent and in a terminal condition or in a state of permanent unconsciousness" (20-§5405).

The Declaration may be revoked "at any time and in any manner by the declarant without regard to the declarant's mental or physical condition. A revocation is effective upon communication to the attending physician or other health care provider by the declarant or a witness to the revocation" (20-§5406).

In addition to the above Declaration Pennsylvania law has devised a system for a Do-Not-Resuscitate (DNR) order to be arranged and contained in a bracelet or necklace issued to the person desiring it. This order is intended to cover those situations where attending health care providers would not have access to a DNR desire, such as emergency responding personnel. Anyone age 18 or who is married if younger, or the person's "surrogate" who has authority to make a decision, can arrange for this. The statute provides the following form to effect this directive:

Pennsylvania Out-of-Hospital
Do-Not-Resuscitate Order

"Patient's full legal name: _____

I, the undersigned, state that I am the attending physician of the patient named above. The above-named patient has requested this order, and I have made the determination that this patient is in a terminal condition and eligible for an order.

I direct any and all emergency medical services personnel, commencing on the effective date of this order, to withhold cardiopulmonary resuscitation (cardiac compression, invasive airway techniques, artificial ventilation, defibrillation and other related procedures) from the patient in the event of the patient's respiratory or cardiac arrest. I further direct such personnel to provide to the patient other medical interventions, such as intravenous fluids, oxygen, or other therapies necessary to provide comfort care or to alleviate pain, unless directed otherwise by the patient or the emergency medical services provider's authorized medical command physician.

Signature of attending physician: _____

Printed name of attending physician: _____

Dated: _____

Attending physician's
emergency telephone number:_____

I, the undersigned, hereby direct that in the event of my cardiac and/or respiratory arrest, efforts at cardiopulmonary resuscitation not be initiated. I understand that I may revoke these directions at any time by giving verbal instructions to the emergency medical services providers, by physical cancellation or destruction of this form or my bracelet or necklace, or by simply not displaying this form or the bracelet or necklace for my EMS caregivers.

Signature of patient: _____
(if capable of making informed decisions)

I, the undersigned, hereby certify that I am authorized to execute this order on the patient's behalf by virtue of having been designated as the patient's surrogate and/or by virtue of my relationship to the patient (specify relationship: _____). I hereby direct that in the event of the patient's cardiac and/or respiratory arrest, efforts at cardiopulmonary resuscitation not be initiated."

Signature of surrogate: _____
(if patient is incapable of making informed decisions)

The statute also provides that this order may be revoked by the patient or surrogate.

VIRGINIA ADVANCE MEDICAL DIRECTIVE

(Statutory Form, IC 15-35-4-10)

Author's Note: An advance directive executed pursuant to this article may, but need not, be in the following form. Note there are various options to consider in selection.

I, _____, willfully and voluntarily make known my wishes in the event that I am incapable of making an informed decision, as follows: I understand that my advance directive may include the selection of an agent, as well as set forth my choices regarding health care. The term "health care" means the furnishing of services to any individual for the purpose of preventing, alleviating, curing, or healing human illness, injury, or physical disability, including, but not limited to, medications; surgery; blood transfusions; chemotherapy; radiation therapy; admission to a hospital, assisted living facility, or other health care facility; psychiatric or other mental health treatment; and life-prolonging procedures and palliative care.

The phrase "incapable of making an informed decision" means unable to understand the nature, extent, and probable consequences of a proposed health care decision, or unable to make a rational evaluation of the risks and benefits of a proposed health care decision as compared with the risks and benefits of alternatives to that decision, or unable to communicate such understanding in any way. The determination that I am incapable of making an informed decision shall be made by my attending physician and a second physician or licensed clinical psychologist after a personal examination of me, and shall be certified in writing. The second physician or licensed clinical psychologist shall not be otherwise currently involved in my treatment, unless such independent physician or licensed clinical psychologist is not reasonably available. Such certification shall be required before health care is provided, continued, withheld, or withdrawn, before any named agent shall be granted authority to make health care decisions on my behalf; and before, or as soon as reasonably practicable after, health care is provided, continued, withheld, or withdrawn, and every 180 days thereafter while the need for health care continues.

If, at any time, I am determined to be incapable of making an informed decision, I shall be notified, to the extent I am capable of receiving such notice, that such determination has been made before health care is provided, continued, withheld, or withdrawn. Such notice shall also be provided, as soon as practical, to my named agent or person authorized by § 54.1-2986 to make health care decisions on my behalf. If I am later determined to be capable of making an informed decision by a physician, in writing, upon personal examination, any further health care decisions will require my informed consent.

(SELECT ANY OR ALL OF THE OPTIONS BELOW.)

OPTION I: APPOINTMENT OF AGENT (CROSS THROUGH OPTIONS I AND II BELOW IF YOU DO NOT WANT TO APPOINT AN AGENT TO MAKE HEALTH CARE DECISIONS FOR YOU.)

I hereby appoint _____ (primary agent), of _____ (address and telephone number), as my agent to make health care decisions on my behalf as authorized in this document.

If _____ (primary agent) is not reasonably available or is unable or unwilling to act as my agent, then I appoint _____ (successor agent), of _____ (address and telephone number), to serve in that capacity.

I hereby grant to my agent, named above, full power and authority to make health care decisions on my behalf as described below whenever I have been determined to be incapable of making an informed decision. My agent's authority hereunder is effective as long as I am incapable of making an informed decision.

In exercising the power to make health care decisions on my behalf, my agent shall follow my desires and preferences as stated in this document or as otherwise known to my agent. My agent shall be guided by my medical diagnosis and prognosis and any information provided by my physicians as to the intrusiveness, pain, risks, and side effects associated with treatment or nontreatment. My agent shall not make any decision regarding my health care that he knows, or upon reasonable inquiry ought to know, is contrary to my religious beliefs or my basic values, whether expressed orally or in writing. If my agent cannot determine what health care choice I would have made on my own behalf, then my agent shall make a choice for me based upon what he believes to be in my best interests.

OPTION II: POWERS OF MY AGENT (CROSS THROUGH ANY LANGUAGE YOU DO NOT WANT AND ADD ANY LANGUAGE YOU DO WANT.)

The powers of my agent shall include the following:

A. To consent to or refuse or withdraw consent to any type of health care, treatment, surgical procedure, diagnostic procedure, medication and the use of mechanical or other procedures that affect any bodily function, including, but not limited to, artificial respiration, artificially administered nutrition and hydration, and cardiopulmonary resuscitation. This authorization specifically includes the power to consent to the administration of dosages of pain-relieving medication in excess of recommended dosages in an amount sufficient to relieve pain, even if such medication carries the risk of addiction or of inadvertently hastening my death;

B. To request, receive, and review any information, verbal or written, regarding my physical or mental health, including, but not limited to, medical and hospital records, and to consent to the disclosure of this information;

C. To employ and discharge my health care providers;

D. To authorize my admission to or discharge (including transfer to another facility) from any hospital, hospice, nursing home, assisted living facility, or other medical care facility. If I have authorized admission to a health care facility for treatment of mental illness, that authority is stated elsewhere in this advance directive;

E. To authorize my admission to a health care facility for the treatment of mental illness for no more than 10 calendar days, provided I do not protest the admission; and a physician on the staff of or designated by the proposed admitting facility examines me and states in writing that I have a mental illness and I am incapable of making an informed decision about my admission, and that I need treatment in the facility; and to authorize my discharge (including transfer to another facility) from the facility;

F.   To authorize my admission to a health care facility for the treatment of mental illness for no more than 10 calendar days, even over my protest, if a physician on the staff of or designated by the proposed admitting facility examines me and states in writing that I have a mental illness and I am incapable of making an informed decision about my admission, and that I need treatment in the facility; and to authorize my discharge (including transfer to another facility) from the facility. My physician or licensed clinical psychologist hereby attests that I am capable of making an informed decision and that I understand the consequences of this provision of my advance directive: _____

_____);

G.   To authorize the specific types of health care identified in this advance directive (specify cross-reference to other sections of directive), even over my protest. My physician or licensed clinical psychologist hereby attests that I am capable of making an informed decision and that I understand the consequences of this provision of my advance directive: _____);

H.   To continue to serve as my agent even in the event that I protest the agent's authority after I have been determined to be incapable of making an informed decision;

I. To authorize my participation in any health care study approved by an institutional review board or research review committee according to applicable federal or state law that offers the prospect of direct therapeutic benefit to me;

J. To authorize my participation in any health care study approved by an institutional review board or research review committee pursuant to applicable federal or state law that aims to increase scientific understanding of any condition that I may have or otherwise to promote human well-being, even though it offers no prospect of direct benefit to me;

K. To make decisions regarding visitation during any time that I am admitted to any health care facility, consistent with the following directions: _____
_____; and

L. To take any lawful actions that may be necessary to carry out these decisions, including the granting of releases of liability to medical providers.

Further, my agent shall not be liable for the costs of health care pursuant to his or her authorization, based solely on that authorization.

OPTION III: HEALTH CARE INSTRUCTIONS (CROSS THROUGH PARAGRAPHS A AND/OR B IF YOU DO NOT WANT TO GIVE ADDITIONAL SPECIFIC INSTRUCTIONS ABOUT YOUR HEALTH CARE.)

A. I specifically direct that I receive the following health care if it is medically appropriate under the circumstances as determined by my attending physician: _____

_____

B. I specifically direct that the following health care not be provided to me under the following circumstances (you may specify that certain health care not be provided under any circumstances): _____

_____

OPTION IV: END-OF-LIFE INSTRUCTIONS (CROSS THROUGH THIS OPTION IF YOU DO NOT WANT TO GIVE INSTRUCTIONS ABOUT YOUR HEALTH CARE IF YOU HAVE A TERMINAL CONDITION.)

If at any time my attending physician should determine that I have a terminal condition where the application of life-prolonging procedures — including artificial respiration, cardiopulmonary resuscitation, artificially administered nutrition, and artificially administered hydration — would serve only to artificially prolong the dying process, I direct that such procedures be withheld or withdrawn, and that I be permitted to die naturally with only the administration of medication or the performance of any medical procedure deemed necessary to provide me with comfort care or to alleviate pain.

OPTION: OTHER DIRECTIONS ABOUT LIFE-PROLONGING PROCEDURES. (If you wish to provide your own directions, or if you wish to add to the directions you have given above, you may do so here. If you wish to give specific instructions regarding certain life-prolonging procedures, such as artificial respiration, cardiopulmonary resuscitation, artificially administered nutrition, and artificially administered hydration, this is where you should write them.) I direct that: _____

_____

_____

_____

_____

OPTION: My other instructions regarding my care if I have a terminal condition are as follows: _____

_____

_____

_____

_____

In the absence of my ability to give directions regarding the use of such life-prolonging procedures, it is my intention that this advance directive shall be honored by my family and physician as the final expression of my legal right to refuse health care and acceptance of the consequences of such refusal.

OPTION V: APPOINTMENT OF AN AGENT TO MAKE AN ANATOMICAL GIFT OR ORGAN, TISSUE, OR EYE DONATION (CROSS THROUGH IF YOU DO NOT WANT TO APPOINT AN AGENT TO MAKE AN ANATOMICAL GIFT OR ANY ORGAN, TISSUE, OR EYE DONATION FOR YOU.)

Upon my death, I direct that an anatomical gift of all of my body or certain organ, tissue or eye donations may be made pursuant to Article 2 (§ 32.1-289.2 et seq.) of Chapter 8 of Title 32.1 and in accordance with my directions, if any.

I hereby appoint _____ as my agent, of _____ (address and telephone number), to make any such anatomical gift or organ, tissue, or eye donation following my death. I further direct that: _____ _____ (declarant's directions concerning anatomical gift or organ, tissue, or eye donation).

This advance directive shall not terminate in the event of my disability.

AFFIRMATION AND RIGHT TO REVOKE:

By signing below, I indicate that I am emotionally and mentally capable of making this advance directive and that I understand the purpose and effect of this document. I understand I may revoke all or any part of this document at any time:

(i) with a signed, dated writing;

(ii) by physical cancellation or destruction of this advance directive by myself, or by directing someone else to destroy it in my presence; or

(iii) by my oral expression of intent to revoke.

_____   _____
(Date)   (Signature of Declarant)

The declarant signed the foregoing advance directive in my presence.

(Witness) _____

(Witness) _____

Appendix C

Estate Planning Worksheets

The following worksheets are intended to assist you with organizing other information for planning your estate. There are many aspects to planning estate planning, and the process begins with the POA forms you have been reading about throughout this book. After you have prepared your POA, consider moving on to other aspects of your estate, such as making your will or forming a trust. The worksheets in this appendix will help you to organize your personal information in preparation for beginning the estate planning process. Planning your estate requires gathering information regarding all aspects of your life, including your personal biographical information, details on assets, and funeral wishes. Preparing a complete estate planning may require the assistance of an attorney, depending on your circumstances. Gathering the required information before consulting legal council can save you time and money from expensive legal fees.

You will have a number of true/false (T/F) questions, multiple-choice questions, and fill-in-the-blank questions.

1. Estate planning requires an attorney.

   ❑ *True*   ❑ *False*

2. You are required to be embalmed when you are being buried.

   ❑ *True*   ❑ *False*

3. You are required to buy a casket at the funeral home you have chosen to use.

   ❑ *True*   ❑ *False*

4. If you are cremated, you are not allowed to have your ashes scattered in a public place.

   ❑ *True*   ❑ *False*

5. If you have property transferred to a trust, it must still go through probate.

   ❑ *True*   ❑ *False*

6. There is no such thing as an oral will.

   ❑ *True*   ❑ *False*

7. You have to pay taxes on any monetary gifts you give, no matter the amount.

   ❑ *True*   ❑ *False*

8. A doctor has to follow your medical directives.

❏ *True*   ❏ *False*

9. A will must be typed and signed in order to be valid.

❏ *True*   ❏ *False*

10. You must state whom you want as a guardian in your will.

❏ *True*   ❏ *False*

11. Once you have your will and durable power of attorney done, regardless of where you may move, it is valid in all 50 states and the District of Columbia.

❏ *True*   ❏ *False*

12. A _____ proceeding is required with a will.

    A. trust

    B. will

    C. probate

    D. none of the above

13. A(n) _____ is a trust that allows you to bypass probate hearings concerning a particular property.

    A. irrevocable land trust

    B. revocable living trust

    C. time-stamped trust

    D. none of the above

14. The creation of a _____ is possible with the carbon from cremation ashes.

   A. model

   B. diamond

   C. clone

   D. none of the above

15. You can _____ a casket for a viewing.

   A. steal

   B. hang

   C. rent

   D. none of the above

16. You can lose around _____ percent of your property in probate hearings.

   A. 20

   B. 50

   C. 75

   D. none of the above

17. A _____ is a type of fraternal membership.

   A. Water Buffalo Order

   B. Jaycee

   C. Freemason

   D. none of the above

18. A(n) _____ is another name for a handwritten will.

   A. laser

   B. holographic

C. ethical

D. none of the above

19. You can put a body _____ instead of embalming.

    A. on ice

    B. in a special chemical soup

    C. there is no substitute

    D. none of the above

20. A _____ is a large party to celebrate a person's life.

    A. wake

    B. visitation

    C. viewing

    D. none of the above

21. A _____ allows you to name someone while you are alive to take care of your financial matters, should you become incapacitated.

    A. medical power of attorney

    B. durable power of attorney for finances

    C. revocable living trust

    D. none of the above

22. A(n) _____ is a set of instructions of what to do if you should become incapacitated and unable to make medical decisions.

23. A(n) _____ is in charge of handling your affairs after you die.

24. A(n) _____ agreement occurs before a couple is married and can impact a person's estate.

25. A(n) _____ trust allows a couple to pass on their estate only after both spouses have died. It is a trust that helps prevent federal estate taxes from being levied.

26. It is a good idea to assign someone to care for your pet. There are some _____ schools that will take them in and take care of them.

27. What assets escape probate without any real action on your part? _____

28. _____ donation can be done for medical research at a university.

29. A(n) _____ is a place where urns can be stored.

30. A(n) _____ account is a bank account that can allow funds to be released upon your death.

31. A(n) _____ is someone who is chosen to carry a casket.

32. Being _____ is a state in which you cannot make decisions for yourself.

33. Does everyone pay estate taxes?

34. Can I simply gift away all my possessions before I die?

35. Is it possible to make a change to an irrevocable trust that has already been established?

36. Can a parent sign legal documents, handle business affairs, or make medical decisions for their adult children?

37. For Medicaid purposes, is a transfer of not more than $12,000 annually allowed?

38. Does a will completely avoid probate?

39. If both parents die, and there are minor children, who has priority for the judge to pick as guardian?

Your Estate in Black and White

Name _____ Birth _____ SS# _____

Spouse _____ Birth _____ SS# _____

Primary Address _____ # of Minors _____

Child _____ Birth _____ SS# _____

Child _____ Birth _____ SS# _____

Guardian of _____ Birth _____ SS# _____

ASSETS

Real Estate: *primary residence, vacation home, land*

Address/ Description	Ownership	Mortgage(s)	Purchase Price/Year	Current Value

Automobile(s)

Year	Make	Model	Ownership	Current Value

Accounts: *checking, savings, certificate of deposit, brokerage*

Type	Beneficiary(ies)	Account #	Current Value

Life Insurance

Company	Insured	Beneficiary(ies)	Ownership	Face Value	Current Value

Retirement: *401(k), IRA, Roth IRA, Keogh, pension, profit sharing, social security*

Plan	Ownership Current Value	Beneficiary(ies)	Vested Year/ Percent

Other Financial Assets: *stocks, bond, inheritance, structured settlement, rent payments*

Type	Beneficiary(ies)	Ownership	Current Value

Personal Property: *boat/jet ski, jewelry, artwork, antiques, collectibles, household contents, etc.*

Type	Value	Purchase Year	Current Value

ADDITIONAL ASSETS			
List all of the things that did not fit on previous page of the inventory sheet:			
Type	Ownership	Due/Payoff Year	Current Value

$ _____

Total Assets $ _____

LIABILITIES			
First mortgage, second mortgage, line of credit, car loan, and credit card balance, for example			
Type	Ownership	Due/Payoff Year	Current Value

Total Liabilities $ _____

Total Assets $ _____

Total Liabilities — $ _____

Total Net Worth = $ _____

Prioritization

This is about making choices regarding what you can and cannot do with your estate. Indicate your six key values. These are the values or qualities to which you are attracted:

1.	
2.	
3.	
4.	
5.	
6.	

Now list all of the things you would like to accomplish with your estate planning, and connect those with your highest values: If more than one value is accomplished, note that.

		Goals	Value
1.	$5k	Leave a substantial amount of money to cat shelter	Involvement
2.	$50k	Education funds for niece and nephews	Education
3.	$		
4.	$		
5.	$		
6.	$		
7.	$		
8.	$		
9.	$		
10.	$		
11.	$		

After you have completed your list of goals, place an approximate dollar value for the gift you would like to leave in the left-hand margin. Use a range if you are not sure.

Total Gifts $ _____

Who, What, How, and When

After you decide on the people and organizations to receive a bequest, take a moment to write out your list. This will be useful when you sit down with your estate planning team to finalize the paperwork and implementation of your estate plan. Leave any places blank if you are unsure.

Who/ relationship	What Circumstances	How	When	Special
Jeanine/niece	*$50,000 + books ($10k value)*	*Trust (bequest)*	*2008*	*Will*
Cat shelter/charity	*$5,000*	*Bequest*	*2008*	*Will*
Frank/son	*$250,000*	*Living trust/bequest*	*2008*	*Will*

Essential Documents and Accounts Inventory

Life will go on after you die, and handling your estate will likely fall to people who are mired in grief. To make it easier to find and deal with the accounts and obligations you leave behind, consolidate as much information as possible. This worksheet is a place to begin compiling that data.

This information will also be helpful to have when you meet with your estate planner.

DEBTS
Mortgage
Company Name:
Account Number:
Contact:
Phone Number:
E-Mail Address:
Payment Amount:
Usual Due Date:
Method of Payment: *(automatic deductions for checking / savings, on-line bill payment via bank, coupon with check)*
PIN: *(Personal Identification Number)*
Secret Question:
Answer:
Second Mortgage
Company Name:
Account Number:
Contact:
Phone Number:
E-Mail Address:
Payment Amount:
Usual Due Date:
Method of Payment:
PIN:
Secret Question:
Answer:
Timeshare — Mortgage Information
Company Name:
Account Number:

Contact:
Phone Number:
E-Mail Address:
Payment Amount:
Usual Due Date:
Method of Payment:
PIN:
Secret Question:
Answer:
Vacation Property — Mortgage Information
Company Name:
Account Number:
Contact:
Phone Number:
E-Mail Address:
Payment Amount:
Usual Due Date:
Method of Payment:
PIN:
Secret Question:
Answer:
Loans — Home Equity
Company Name:
Account Number:
Contact:
Phone Number:
E-Mail Address:
Payment Amount:
Usual Due Date:
Method of Payment:
PIN:
Secret Question:
Answer:
Loans — Line of Credit
Company Name:
Account Number:
Contact:

Phone Number:
E-Mail Address:
Payment Amount:
Usual Due Date:
Method of Payment:
PIN:
Secret Question:
Answer:
Loans — Signature
Company Name:
Account Number:
Contact:
Phone Number:
E-Mail Address:
Payment Amount:
Usual Due Date:
Method of Payment:
PIN:
Secret Question:
Answer:
Loans — Student/College Tuition
Company Name:
Account Number:
Contact:
Phone Number:
E-Mail Address:
Payment Amount:
Usual Due Date:
Method of Payment:
PIN:
Secret Question:
Answer:
Loans — Automobile
Company Name:
Account Number:
Contact:
Phone Number:

E-Mail Address:
Payment Amount:
Usual Due Date:
Method of Payment:
PIN:
Secret Question:
Answer:
Loans — Other (boat, second car, etc.)
Company Name:
Account Number:
Contact:
Phone Number:
E-Mail Address:
Payment Amount:
Usual Due Date:
Method of Payment:
PIN:
Secret Question:
Answer:
Credit Card #1
Company Name:
Account Number:
Contact:
Phone Number:
E-Mail Address:
Payment Amount:
Usual Due Date:
Method of Payment:
PIN:
Secret Question:
Answer:
Credit Card #2
Company Name:
Account Number:
Contact:
Phone Number:
E-Mail Address:

Payment Amount:
Usual Due Date:
Method of Payment:
PIN:
Secret Question:
Answer:
Credit Card #3
Company Name:
Account Number:
Contact:
Phone Number:
E-Mail Address:
Payment Amount:
Usual Due Date:
Method of Payment:
PIN:
Secret Question:
Answer:
Other — Account 2
Company Name:
Account Number:
Contact:
Phone Number:
E-Mail Address:
Payment Amount:
Usual Due Date:
Method of Payment:
PIN:
Secret Question:
Answer:
Other — Account 2
Company Name:
Account Number:
Contact:
Phone Number:
E-Mail Address:
Payment Amount:

Usual Due Date:
Method of Payment:
PIN:
Secret Question:
Answer:
Other — Account 2
Company Name:
Account Number:
Contact:
Phone Number:
E-Mail Address:
Payment Amount:
Usual Due Date:
Method of Payment:
PIN:
Secret Question:
Answer:
LIVING EXPENSES
Gas and Electric
Company Name:
Account Number:
Contact:
Phone Number:
E-Mail Address:
Payment Amount:
Usual Due Date:
Method of Payment:
PIN:
Secret Question:
Answer:
Water and Sewer or Septic
Company Name:
Account Number:
Contact:
Phone Number:
E-Mail Address:
Payment Amount:

Usual Due Date:	
Method of Payment:	
PIN:	
Secret Question:	
Answer:	
Telephone	
Company Name:	
Account Number:	
Contact:	
Phone Number:	
E-Mail Address:	
Payment Amount:	
Usual Due Date:	
Method of Payment:	
PIN:	
Secret Question:	
Answer:	
Heating Oil	
Company Name:	
Account Number:	
Contact:	
Phone Number:	
E-Mail Address:	
Payment Amount:	
Usual Due Date:	
Method of Payment:	
PIN:	
Secret Question:	
Answer:	
Internet Service Provider (ISP)	
Company Name:	
Account Number:	
Contact:	
Phone Number:	
E-Mail Address:	
Payment Amount:	
Usual Due Date:	

Method of Payment:
PIN:
Secret Question:
Answer:
Cable/Satellite Television Service
Company Name:
Account Number:
Contact:
Phone Number:
E-Mail Address:
Payment Amount:
Usual Due Date:
Method of Payment:
PIN:
Secret Question:
Answer:
Other — Account 2
Company Name:
Account Number:
Contact:
Phone Number:
E-Mail Address:
Payment Amount:
Usual Due Date:
Method of Payment:
PIN:
Secret Question:
Answer:
Other — Account 2
Company Name:
Account Number:
Contact:
Phone Number:
E-Mail Address:
Payment Amount:
Usual Due Date:
Method of Payment:

PIN:	
Secret Question:	
Answer:	
OTHER REGULAR PAYMENTS	
Insurance: Life — Policy 1	
Company Name:	
Account Number:	
Contact:	
Phone Number:	
E-Mail Address:	
Payment Amount:	
Usual Due Date:	
Method of Payment:	
PIN:	
Secret Question:	
Answer:	
Insurance: Life — Policy 2	
Company Name:	
Account Number:	
Contact:	
Phone Number:	
E-Mail Address:	
Payment Amount:	
Usual Due Date:	
Method of Payment:	
PIN:	
Secret Question:	
Answer:	
Insurance: Life — Disability (Long/Short-Term)	
Company Name:	
Account Number:	
Contact:	
Phone Number:	
E-Mail Address:	
Payment Amount:	
Usual Due Date:	
Method of Payment:	

PIN:
Secret Question:
Answer:
Insurance: Life — Homeowner's/Renter's
Company Name:
Account Number:
Contact:
Phone Number:
E-Mail Address:
Payment Amount:
Usual Due Date:
Method of Payment:
PIN:
Secret Question:
Answer:
Insurance: Car — Policy 1
Company Name:
Account Number:
Contact:
Phone Number:
E-Mail Address:
Payment Amount:
Usual Due Date:
Method of Payment:
PIN:
Secret Question:
Answer:
Insurance: Car — Policy 2
Company Name:
Account Number:
Contact:
Phone Number:
E-Mail Address:
Payment Amount:
Usual Due Date:
Method of Payment:
PIN:

Secret Question:	
Answer:	
Newspaper Subscription 1	
Company Name:	
Account Number:	
Contact:	
Phone Number:	
E-Mail Address:	
Payment Amount:	
Usual Due Date:	
Method of Payment:	
Newspaper Subscription 2	
Company Name:	
Account Number:	
Contact:	
Phone Number:	
E-Mail Address:	
Payment Amount:	
Usual Due Date:	
Method of Payment:	
Magazine Subscription 1	
Company Name:	
Account Number:	
Contact:	
Phone Number:	
E-Mail Address:	
Payment Amount:	
Usual Due Date:	
Method of Payment:	
Magazine Subscription 2	
Company Name:	
Account Number:	
Contact:	
Phone Number:	
E-Mail Address:	
Payment Amount:	
Usual Due Date:	

Method of Payment:	
Magazine Subscription 3	
Company Name:	
Account Number:	
Contact:	
Phone Number:	
E-Mail Address:	
Payment Amount:	
Usual Due Date:	
Method of Payment:	
Other — Account 1	
Company Name:	
Account Number:	
Contact:	
Phone Number:	
E-Mail Address:	
Payment Amount:	
Usual Due Date:	
Method of Payment:	
PIN:	
Secret Question:	
Answer:	
Other — Account 2	
Company Name:	
Account Number:	
Contact:	
Phone Number:	
E-Mail Address:	
Payment Amount:	
Usual Due Date:	
Method of Payment:	
PIN:	
Secret Question:	
Answer:	
INCOME	
Payroll Check 1	
Company Name:	

Account Number:	
Contact:	
Phone Number:	
E-Mail Address:	
Check Amount:	
Pay Day/Dates:	
Method of Payment: *(check, direct deposit, cash, other)*	
Additional Important Information:	
Payroll Check 2	
Company Name:	
Account Number:	
Contact:	
Phone Number:	
E-Mail Address:	
Check Amount:	
Pay Day/Dates:	
Method of Payment: *(check, direct deposit, cash, other)*	
Additional Important Information:	
Structured Settlement	
Company Name:	
Account Number:	
Contact:	
Phone Number:	
E-Mail Address:	
Check Amount:	
Day/Dates Paid:	
Method of Payment: *(check, direct deposit, cash, other)*	
Additional Important Information:	
Royalty Payment 1	
Company Name:	
Account Number:	
Contact:	

Phone Number:	
E-Mail Address:	
Check Amount:	
Day/Dates Paid:	
Method of Payment: *(check, direct deposit, cash, other)*	
Additional Important Information:	

Royalty Payment 1	
Company Name:	
Account Number:	
Contact:	
Phone Number:	
E-Mail Address:	
Check Amount:	
Day/Dates Paid:	
Method of Payment: *(check, direct deposit, cash, other)*	
Additional Important Information:	

Royalty Payment 2	
Company Name:	
Account Number:	
Contact:	
Phone Number:	
E-Mail Address:	
Check Amount:	
Day/Dates Paid:	
Method of Payment: *(check, direct deposit, cash, other)*	
Additional Important Information:	

Annuity Payment 1	
Company Name:	
Account Number:	
Contact:	
Phone Number:	
E-Mail Address:	

Check Amount	
Day/Dates Paid	
Method of Payment: *(check, direct deposit, cash, other)*	
Additional Important Information:	
Annuity Payment 2	
Company Name:	
Account Number:	
Contact:	
Phone Number:	
E-Mail Address:	
Check Amount	
Day/Dates Paid	
Method of Payment: *(check, direct deposit, cash, other)*	
Additional Important Information:	
Retirement Distribution — Plan 1	
Company Name:	
Account Number:	
Contact:	
Phone Number:	
E-Mail Address:	
Check Amount	
Day/Dates Paid	
Method of Payment: *(check, direct deposit, cash, other)*	
Additional Important Information:	
Retirement Distribution — Plan 2	
Company Name:	
Account Number:	
Contact:	
Phone Number:	
E-Mail Address:	
Check Amount	
Day/Dates Paid	

Method of Payment: *(check, direct deposit, cash, other)*	
Rental Property 1	
Company Name:	
Account Number:	
Contact:	
Phone Number:	
E-Mail Address:	
Check Amount	
Day/Dates Paid	
Method of Payment: *(check, direct deposit, cash, other)*	
Tenant Information:	
Rental Property 2	
Company Name:	
Account Number:	
Contact:	
Phone Number:	
E-Mail Address:	
Check Amount	
Day/Dates Paid	
Method of Payment: *(check, direct deposit, cash, other)*	
Tenant Information:	
FINANCIAL RESOURCES	
Checking — Account 1	
Financial Institution:	
Account Number:	
Contact:	
Phone Number:	
E-Mail Address:	
Balance:	
Date:	
PIN:	
Secret Question:	
Answer:	

Additional Important Information:
Checking — Account 2
Financial Institution:
Account Number:
Contact:
Phone Number:
E-Mail Address:
Balance:
Date:
PIN:
Secret Question:
Answer:
Additional Important Information:
Savings — Account 1
Financial Institution:
Account Number:
Contact:
Phone Number:
E-Mail Address:
Balance:
Date:
PIN:
Secret Question:
Answer:
Additional Important Information:
Savings — Account 2
Financial Institution;
Account Number:
Contact:
Phone Number:
E-Mail Address:
Balance:
Date:
PIN:
Secret Question:

Answer:
Additional Important Information:

Certificate of Deposit – Account 1
Financial Institution:
Account Number:
Contact:
Phone Number:
E-Mail Address:
Balance:
Date:
PIN:
Secret Question:
Answer:
Additional Important Information:

Certificate of Deposit – Account 2
Financial Institution:
Account Number:
Contact:
Phone Number:
E-Mail Address:
Balance:
Date:
PIN:
Secret Question:
Answer:
Additional Important Information:

Money Market Fund – Account 1
Financial Institution:
Account Number:
Contact:
Phone Number:
E-Mail Address:
Balance:
Date:

PIN:
Secret Question:
Answer:
Additional Important Information:
Money Market Fund – Account 2
Financial Institution:
Account Number:
Contact:
Phone Number:
E-Mail Address:
Balance:
Date:
PIN:
Secret Question:
Answer:
Additional Important Information:
Other — Account 1
Financial Institution:
Account Number:
Contact:
Phone Number:
E-Mail Address:
Balance:
Date:
PIN:
Secret Question:
Answer:
Additional Important Information:
Other — Account 2
Financial Institution:
Account Number:
Contact:
Phone Number:
E-Mail Address:

Balance:
Date:
PIN:
Secret Question:
Answer:
Additional Important Information:

Anything that did not fit in a predetermined category: _____

_____

_____

_____

_____

Party Planning with an Unusual Twist

Whether you prefer a traditional and dignified ceremony, or an occasion that is a reflection of how you lived your life, the arrangements for the last event you will attend on earth in this lifetime can be up to you. But you need to make the necessary arrangements, or direct others to do as you wish. *This is not a legally binding document; a lawyer will need to be consulted for the correct language and paperwork.*

Check all that apply (leave blank those things you do not want) and provide any details that are needed.

Your body:

☐ I want my body to be donated to medicine and used for the following purposes: _____

_____

☐ Release the final report, including all test results, to my executor/personal representative: _____
_____

☐ Conduct a post-mortem examination if the following circumstances occur: _____
_____

☐ Cremate my remains, and disposal of my ashes should be conducted as follows: _____
_____

☐ I request a burial to take place in this way: _____
_____

Your service:

☐ I want a memorial service without a casket.

☐ I want a funeral without a casket.

☐ Memorial service with a casket conducted in the following manner:

 ☐ Closed
 ☐ Open
 ☐ Funeral home/mortuary: _____
 Address: _____
 Phone: _____

☐ I would like a funeral service conducted in the following manner:

 Place of worship: _____
 Address: _____

Phone: _____

Presiding clergy: _____

Soloist: _____

Hymns: _____

_____

Musical selections: _____

_____

Musical instruments: _____

_____

Scripture, poem(s), and other materials to be included: _

_____

_____

Other instructions: _____

_____

_____

_____

_____

_____

Memorial gifts should be suggested for the following: __

_____

_____

_____

Other information:

Signed: _____ Date: _____

Estate Plan Summary Sheet

There are many components that can go into an estate plan, but there are some basic documents that most people have. This is a brief inventory that can serve as a checklist for making sure you get all necessary details accomplished.

Use the blank lines to add other documents, such as a prenuptial agreement, that will affect your estate plan.

Estate Plan Components	Deadline	Done On	Notes
Estate Plan Summary Sheet			
Will			
Living Will			
Organ Donor Form/Card			
Durable Power of Attorney			
Medical Power of Attorney			
Guardians for Children			
Guardians for Others			
Life Insurance Policies			
Trust — for Children			
Trust — for Retirement			
Trust — for Charity _____			
Trust — for Charity _____			
Trust — Living			

Retirement — 401(k)/Pension			

Use the Notes sections as reminders for additional information that is needed before the next review. For example, "Get name of Peace Center lawyer" to make sure you have a contact for the charitable trust documents that might need to get to the organization.

Annual To-Do List

Once your estate plan is complete, this list will need to be customized to include each component.

Use the blank lines to add other documents, such as a prenuptial agreement, that will affect your estate plan.

Estate Plan Pieces	Meeting Date	Changes Needed
Estate Plan Summary Sheet		
Will		
Living Will		
Organ Donor Form/Card		
Durable Power of Attorney		
Medical Power of Attorney		
Guardians for Children		
Guardians for Others		
Life Insurance Policies		
Trust — _____		

Trust — _____		
Trust — _____		
Trust — _____		
Retirement — _____		
Retirement — _____		

Estate Planning Quiz Answers

Here you will find the answers to the estate planning quiz you took at the beginning of Appendix C.

1. **F** — While it does not require one, there are some aspects in which an attorney is recommended.

2. **F** — There is no federal law that requires that a body be embalmed. Putting a body in a freezer will preserve it for a few days until a funeral.

3. **F** — There is no law requiring you to buy anything from a funeral home. While they offer such items as caskets, you are not required to buy them.

4. **F** — You may want to check with local laws, but you are allowed to scatter them in most public places.

5. **F** — This allows you to bypass probate.

6. **F** — There is an oral will, but it is not as binding as a signed one and can lead to problems in some areas and states.

7. **F** — It must be over a certain amount before you pay taxes on the money.

8. **F** — They may refuse to follow the directives, but you would then get a new doctor.

9. **F** — It can be oral, but it is not recommended.

10. **F** — If you do not, the court system will choose one for your children.

11. **F** — Every state has specific rules. A will or a durable power of attorney that is valid in one state could be void in another. Check with an attorney in your new state.

12. C

13. B

14. B

15. C

16. D

17. C

18. B

19. A

20. A

21. B

22. Medical directive

23. Executor

24. Marital or prenuptial

25. AB

26. Veterinary

27. Real estate, IRAs, and 401(k) plans, which pass by beneficiary designation under the plan itself; life insurance, which again passes by beneficiary designation together with any payable-on-death accounts, which would pass directly to whoever is designated as a beneficiary; as well as joint accounts, which would pass by right of survivorship to the designated survivor.

28. Whole body

29. Columbarium

30. TOD or transfer on death

31. Pallbearer

32. Incapacitated

33. No. Estate taxes are only imposed on individuals who have estates sufficiently large to trigger the tax.

34. No. The estate tax is tied up with the gift tax so that if you gift all your belongings before death, you might end up paying the same in the gift tax as you would simply leaving your property alone.

35. Yes, there are various ways, including:

    • Petitioning the court to make the desired change.

    • Forming a new irrevocable trust with the desired change and having it purchase the assets from the existing irrevocable trust using an IOU that would be paid off at death, possibly from life insurance proceeds.

- When setting up an irrevocable trust, provide for a "protector" to be able to make a change. The protector cannot be the grantor, trustee, or beneficiary of the trust. It is someone who is named when the trust is formed and given the powers to make certain changes. Typically, you would name someone you trust, such as a family member (e.g., sister or brother) or a professional, such as your attorney or CPA. The protector cannot benefit themselves, but can only make changes as authorized by you, as grantor, when the trust is first established.

36. No. Once an individual reaches the age of majority (typically 18), the adult child should execute powers of attorney for financial and business affairs, as well as their advanced legal directives. For example, an adult child heading off to college may want to execute the health care and financial documents so that if something happened to the child while at college, the parent would have the legal power to assist and make decisions.

37. No. The $12,000 annual gift tax exclusion is strictly a gift tax provision. Medicaid penalizes gifts of any size.

38. No. Not without a power of attorney, conservatorship, or letters testamentary.

39. Generally a grandparent. That knowledge alone could scare some people into getting their documents done.

Glossary of Terms

Advance Directive — Any legally executed and recognized document or oral statement that gives directions for personal health care. Included in this broad term are health care POAs, living wills, and anatomical gift forms.

Affidavit — A written statement of facts as sworn to by an individual before a notary public or clerk of court.

Agent — In the context of POAs, this is another term for attorney-in-fact.

Anatomical Gift — Donation of your body, parts of your body, or organs for the purposes of transplants and medical research, following your death.

Attorney-at-Law — An individual licensed to practice law within a given jurisdiction. This designation is entirely different from an attorney-in-fact.

Attorney-in-Fact — An individual named in a POA document as the one designated to have responsibility for the affairs of another person. Not in any way licensed to practice law, an attorney-in-fact is a person identified to represent the interests of the principal.

Beneficiary — A beneficiary is someone or a group that benefits from the gifts made under a legal document, which can include wills, trusts, pay-on-death accounts, retirement plans, and insurance products. This is the person who gets something from these documents.

Code Blue — A term used by medics to describe a situation of cardiac or respiratory arrest in which all measures have been applied in the effort to resuscitate.

Community Property — Property that is shared between you and your spouse, in a community living state. This property belongs equally to both parties, as it was obtained during the marriage.

Conservator — Another word for "guardian."

Creditor — Any party to whom money is owed.

Debtor — Any party who owes money to another.

Decedent — Reference to the person who has died.

Do-Not-Resuscitate   (DNR) Order — A written statement, signed by the principal or the principal's representative and the principal's doctor, with instructions that medical personnel are not to attempt resuscitation if the principal's heart or breathing stops.

Durable POA — A POA document that remains in effect even if the principal becomes incapacitated.

Estate — All the property that you own when you die is your estate. There are various ways of determining the value of your estate, as defined in this book, including your probate estate and your taxable estate.

Estate Planning — Planning for what will happen to your estate when you die while you are still alive. It helps you move your estate from your property to that of your heirs in the best manner possible.

Execute — In a legal context, this word means to sign a document to make it effective with all required signatures.

Executor — The individual who will manage your estate, move through probate, and collect all your assets. He or she will distribute them to your heirs as you define in your will.

Fiduciary — A term describing the duties of an attorney-in-fact, who is obligated and trusted to act in the interests of the principal, as if the attorney-in-fact were the principal.

Financial POA — This term differentiates a POA executed for the purpose of business and financial affairs, as opposed to one executed for health care purposes.

General POA — The basic document, this form allows extremely broad powers to be assigned to the agent; it is often used to facilitate business management.

Guardian — If a person is judged incompetent, and he or she has not executed any advance directives, eventually the court will assign a guardian to oversee that person's affairs.

Grantor — A grantor is a person that establishes a trust.

Health Care POA — A durable POA completed for the purpose of assigning someone to represent the principal in health care issues, in the event of the principal's incapacity.

Heirs — Those who will inherit property, by law, at the time of death of those they are related to. Heirs will receive property that is not left specifically through a will or trust to someone else.

Holographic Will — Last will and testament completely written in the decedent's own handwriting, signed and dated but not required to be witnessed, legal only in those states that recognize such a will form.

Hydration — The administration of liquids via an intravenous or gastrointestinal tube to a person who is not able to swallow sufficient amounts of water.

Incapacity — Mental inability to understand information or make decisions, or mental or physical inability to communicate.

Incompetence — A considered judgment rendered by the courts stating that an individual is not capable of handling his or her own affairs: a legally determined recognition of incapacity.

Instrument — A term for a formal legal document.

Insurance — A product that is purchased that provides protection from a variety of situations in the event that they happen. Life insurance, for ex-

ample, provides coverage in a monetary benefit if the insured person dies while the policy is in effect.

Joint Tenancy — When two or more people own property, the other will become the owner of the entire property when one dies.

Letter of Attorney — Another term for power of attorney.

Life-Prolonging Medical Procedure — Treatments administered for the sole purpose of prolonging life and not addressing the causes or cures of any affliction. Examples of these are defibrillation, respirators, and tubal nutrition and hydration.

Limited POA — As opposed to a general POA, this version is in some way circumscribed, with a time, purpose, and/or jurisdiction that is limited as specifically stated in the document.

Living Trust — A relationship created between a principal and an agent, in which the principal's assets are transferred to the agent who is entrusted with them for the benefit of a third party. The document is created while the principal is living, and often names the principal as the beneficiary until death, after which time the assets transfer to the third party. A living trust typically includes a health care POA and other advance directives.

Living Will — A witnessed document in which the principal specifies directives for end-of-life treatment, should the principal not be in a position to understand the situation, make decisions, or communicate.

Notary Public — A person certified by the state to administer oaths; that is, to provide certification as to the identity of the principal and the fact of the signing.

Notary Acknowledgement — The portion of a legal document that is completed by the notary public.

Nutrition (Artificial) — Sustenance delivered to a patient either intravenously or via a tube directly inserted into the stomach or intestine (gastrointestinal) or via a tube inserted through the nostrils (nasogastric).

Palliative Care — Health care for patients that is concerned with relieving pain and increasing comfort, rather than with treatments or cures.

Persistent Vegetative State — Resulting from brain damage, this condition is one of continued unresponsiveness, without control of cognition or voluntary movement. The patient exhibits sleep-wake cycles and continues breathing, but is unlikely to regain consciousness. After some time in this condition, the patient is said to be in a permanent vegetative state (PVS) with no hope of recovery.

Probate — Probate is a process that includes several steps. Probate authenticates the will of the deceased, appoints the executor or administrator of your will, pays debts and taxes that are due on the estate, identifies whom the heirs of the estate are, and distributes the property in the will to those who are designated in the will.

Proxy — Yet another word for attorney-in-fact.

Power of Attorney — The document used to confer responsibilities from the principal to the chosen attorney-in-fact. The term also refers to the actual powers themselves that are conferred. In either case, the plural of the term is powers of attorney (not power of attorneys.)

Principal — The first party in a POA document; the person who names another person to be his or her attorney-in-fact.

Resuscitation — Reviving someone, either by manual or mechanical methods, after he or she has stopped breathing.

Revocation — A statement that withdraws powers and

privileges assigned previously in a POA.

Springing POA — A POA that specifically does not take effect until a certain time occurs, or certain circumstances are in place.

Surrogate — One more of the many terms for an attorney-in-fact, a trusted representative who is named in your POA document.

Terminal Condition — Not easy to define, this most often refers to a condition judged by at least two physicians to be beyond cure, and that will result in death if no life-prolonging measures are applied. Some people may limit the meaning to apply to only those situations when even with life-prolonging measures, the patient is likely to die soon. A term to approach cautiously; make sure you understand how it is used in any document you sign.

Third Party — The parties (the people or legal entities) involved in completing your POA are you, an attorney-in-fact, and anyone the attorney-in-fact may encounter in the process of carrying out the duties prescribed in the document. This last party is the third party. Looked at another way, anyone who is not the principal or the attorney-in-fact is a third party.

Trust — A legal document and situation in which property is held for the benefit of others. The grantor or trustor places property into the trust that is managed by the trustee until it passes to the beneficiary.

Trustee — The trustee of a trust is the person that will manage the trust for the beneficiary until they can take claim to the property in it.

Trustor — The creator of a trust.

Uniform Laws — The National Conference of Commissioners on Uniform State Laws works to draft laws that are broadly applicable for use anywhere in the United States. It is up to each state whether to adopt these versions of legislation Many states have enacted all or part of the Uniform Health Care Decisions Act approved by Congress in 1993; other states either already have in place their own laws about advance directives, or are currently in the process of creating them.

Will — A will is a legal document that defines what the deceased person's wishes are in regard to his or her property. It provides for what their intentions are for where property should go after they die.

Bibliography

Alexander, George J., *Writing a Living Will Using a Durable Power of Attorney*, Preager Publishers, New York, NY, 1988.

www.anatomicalgiftact.org.

"Attorney," **www.etymoline.com**.

"The Aural (auditory-musical-rhythmic) learning style," **www.learning-styles-online.com/style/aural-auditory-musical/**.

Brotman, Barbara, "Understanding fear of death," *Chicago Tribune*, November 20, 2006.

Burke, Casey, Social Worker, Personal Interview, October 4, 2008.

"Cardiopulmonary resuscitation (CPR): First aid," **www.mayoclinic.com/health/first-aid-cpr/FA00061**.

Cebuhar, Jo Kline, *Last Things First, Just in Case*, Murphy Publishing, Des Moines, IA, 2006.

"Certified First Responder," **http://en.wikipedia.org/wiki/Certified_first_responder**.

"Court and the End of Life - The Right To Privacy: Karen Ann Quinlan," **www.libraryindex.com/pages/582/Court-End-Life-RIGHT-PRIVACY-KAREN-ANN-QUINLAN.html**.

"Cruzan v Director, Missouri Department of Health," **www.law.umkc.edu/faculty/projects/ftrials/conlaw/cruzan.html**.

Distenfield, Ira, Linda Distenfield, *We The People's Guide to Estate Planning*, John Wiley & Sons, Inc., Hoboken, NJ, 2006.

Downes, Kim, Registered Nurse, Personal Interview, May 15, 2008.

Dunbar, Karen APRN, BC, *NurseWeek*, 2004.

Dyer, Kristi A., MD, MS, FT, "Karen Ann Quinlan - A Focal Point for Death with Dignity/Right to Die Movement," **http://dying.about.com**.

Dyer, Sue, "The Root Causes of Poor Communication," **www.myarticlearchive.com**.

Editorial Staff, "Panic Attacks, Panic Disorder and Agoraphobia," **www.familydoctor.org**.

Ekroth, Loren Ph.D., "High Time to Change Childish Conversation," **www.hodu.com/childish.shtml**.

"Emotional Intelligence," **http://en.wikipedia.org/wiki/Emotional_intelligence**.

"Fear," **www.dictionary.com**.

George Washington Papers at the Library of Congress, 1741-1799: Series 4. General Correspondence. 1697-1799

Greene, Miss Mary A., "Legal Condition of Woman 1492-1892," Mary Kavanaugh Oldham Eagle, ed., *The Congress of Women: Held in the Woman's Building, World's Columbian Exposition, Chicago, U. S. A.*, 1893., Chicago, IL: Monarch Book Company, 1894. pp. 41-52, at **http://74.125.93.132/search?q=cache:WhEfYyUMfPwJ:digital.library.upenn.edu/women/eagle/congress/greene.html+%22Power+of+attorney%22+in+ancient+Rome&cd=40&hl=en&ct=clnk&gl=us.**

Halsall, Paul, *Ancient History Sourcebook: A Collection of Contracts from Mesopotamia*, c. 2300 - 428 BCE, at http://**www.fordham.edu/halsall/ancient/mesopotamia-contracts.html#Power%20of%20Attorney**.

Haman, Edward, *Power of Attorney Handbook*, Sphinx Publishing, Naperville, IL, 2006.

"How To Create a Durable Power of Attorney For Financial Matters," **www.medlawplus.com**.

"How to Deliver Bad News," **www.nfib.com/object/1583889.html**.

Inmon, Julie, Personal Interview, October 1, 2008.

Jackson, Donna J., President and Attorney, Personal Interview, May 9, 2008.

Johns, Claude Hermann Walter, *Babylonian and Assyrian Laws, Contracts and Letters* (New York: Charles Scribner's Sons, 1904), at **http://oll.libertyfund.org/?option=com_staticxt&staticfile=show.php%3Ftitle=2227&chapter=209146&layout=html&Itemid=27**.

Jones, Nathan, Registered Nurse, Personal Interview September 29, 2008.

Kent, Rick, *Paralegal*, October 6, 2008.

"The Legacy of Nancy Cruzan," **www.healthsystem.virginia.edu/internet/him/nancycruzan.cfm**.

"Limited Non-durable Power of Attorney for Minor Child(ren) Care," **www.legalhelpmate.com/power-of-attorney-limited-child-care-nd.aspx**.

Long, Tony, "June 11, 1985: Karen Quinlan Dies, But the Issue Lives On," **www.wired.com**.

McCollum, Chuck, Personal Interview, October 2, 2008.

"Medical Ventilator," **http://en.wikipedia.org/wiki/Medical_ventilator**.

"Nancy Cruzan," **http://en.wikipedia.org/wiki/Nancy_Cruzan**.

"Nancy Cruzan Biography (Medical Patient)," **www.infoplease.com/biography/var/nancycruzan.html**.

"Optimising use of ventilators to treat patients while minimising risk of injury," **www.news-medical.net**.

"Organ donation: Don't let these 10 myths confuse you," **www.mayo-clinic.com**.

Preidt, Robert, "Silver-Coated Ventilator Tubes Cut Risk of Pneumonia," **www.hoc.ch**.

Reichel, William, M.D., *Planning for Uncertainty*, The Johns Hopkins University Press, Baltimore, MD, 2007.

"Rigor Mortis and Other Postmortem Changes," **www.deathreference.com**.

Robinson, Maisah, PhD., "How to Improve your Interpersonal Communication Skills," **www.associatedcontent.com**.

Sherman, Ruth, "Understanding Your Communication Style," **www.au.af.mil/au/awc/awcgate/sba/comm_style.htm**.

Sittenfeld, Curtis, "Good Ways to Deliver Bad News," **www.fastcompany.com**.

Sitarz, Daniel, *Powers of Attorney Simplified*, Nova Publishing Company, 2008.

Smith, Melinda, M.A., "Panic Attacks and Panic Disorder, Symptoms, Causes and Treatment" **www.helpguide.org**.

Stiegel, Lori A., "Durable Power of Attorney Abuse: It's A Crime Too," American Bar Association 2008, at **www.abanet.org/aging/**

about/pdfs/durable_poa_abuse_fact_sheet_criminal_justice_professionals.pdf.

"Symptoms of Fear," http://apps.sdhc.k12.fl.us/public/mainindex/crisis/symptoms.htm.

"Ten Ways to Improve Your Communication Style," www.typepad.com/t/trackback/219222/2440156.

"Terri Schiavo," http://en.wikipedia.org/wiki/Terri_Schiavo.

Texas A&M University, Sons of DeWitt Colony Texas Documents, DeWitt Power of Attorney at www.tamu.edu/ccbn/dewitt/Petition.htm.

Whitaker, Pam, Personal Interview, October 1, 2008.

Widener, Chris, "Getting Over Fear and On with Your Life," www.personal-development.com/articles/getting-over-fear.htm.

Author Biography

L inda C. Ashar, attorney at law, is a lawyer, educator, horse breeder, freelance writer, and artist. Her law practice encompasses of more than 29 years before the Ohio and Federal Bars. She is a senior shareholder in the firm of Wickens, Herzer, Panza, Cook & Batista Co. in Avon, Ohio. In addition to her juris doctor in law, she has a master's of arts in special education and bachelor's of arts in English.

She is a professional writer and has authored *101 Ways to Score Higher on Your LSAT: What You Need to Know About the Law School Admission Test Explained Simply* (Atlantic Publishing Group, Inc. 2008), poetry, and several magazine and journal articles.

She is an adjunct professor at DeVry University and a frequent speaker at law seminars.

She and her lawyer-husband, Mike, operate Thornapple Farms in Vermilion, Ohio, where they breed Morgan Horses, including rare Lippitt Morgan bloodstock, Connemara Ponies, and Irish Kerry Bog Ponies, a critically endangered breed. Ashar serves on several nonprofit boards and is co-founder of Elysian Fields: The Justin Morgan Association for Retired Equines and the American Kerry Bog Pony Society.

Her interpretive art has been showcased by Mac Worthington Gallery in Columbus, Ohio; she paints by private commission, with subjects including equines, portraits and landscapes. Reach her at ashar@hbr.net or lashar@wickenslaw.com.

Index

A

Affidavit of attorney-in-fact, 184, 120, 141

Agency, 192, 15, 18-20, 22

All-in-one POA, 43-44, 154

Anatomical gift form, 126, 140

Artificial feeding, 107

C

Cardio pulmonary resuscitation, 110

Childcare POA, 38, 46, 72-74

Coma, 39, 41, 89, 91-92, 104-107, 117, 138

CPR, 301, 89, 98, 102, 110, 112

D

Defibrillation, 241, 98, 110-112, 296

DNR, 240, 173-175, 41, 92, 122, 125-126, 139-140, 294

Do-not-resuscitate, 240-241, 41, 120, 125, 294

Doctor, 231, 255, 289, 307, 179, 48-50, 68, 103, 107, 113, 116, 125, 127-128, 140, 294

Durable POA, 198, 306, 34, 44-45, 78, 84, 88, 151, 157, 294-295

E

Estate planning, 193, 253-254, 262-263, 289, 302, 36, 143, 294

F

Federal Patient Self-Determination Act, 162

Fiduciary responsibility, 54, 23

Fiduciary responsibility, 54, 23

Financial POA, 203, 207, 166-167, 179, 38, 42-43, 46, 50, 52-55, 76-77, 84, 153-155, 157-162, 295,

G

General POA, 45, 78-79, 295-296

H

Health care POA, 187-188, 166, 170, 179, 38-41, 46, 49-50, 52, 55, 60, 66, 81, 87, 100-101, 103, 117, 121, 124, 149, 153-156, 162, 295, 297

Health Insurance Portability and Accountability Act, 55

HIPAA, 55

Holographic will, 135, 295

J

Jack Kevorkian, 99

K

Karen Ann Quinlan, 302, 88-89

L

Last will and testament, 129, 131-133, 136, 140, 295

Life-sustaining therapies, 106

Limited POA, 42, 45, 73-74, 77-82, 296

Living trust, 255, 257, 263, 173, 120, 129-132, 136, 149, 296-297

M

Mutual will, 135

N

Nancy Cruzan, 304, 88, 90

Notary, 197, 202, 216, 231, 237, 34-35, 177-180, 135, 145, 151, 293, 297, 16, 18, 20, 23

Notary block, 151

O

Organ donation, 305, 127-128

P

Parental consent, 38

Persistent vegetative state, 89, 91-95, 102, 104, 107, 117, 123, 138, 297

Proxy, 192, 208, 33, 42, 48, 298

PVS, 104-105, 297

R

Real estate, 183, 186, 192, 211, 260, 291, 76, 78-80, 84, 147, 29, 16

Revocable living trust, 255, 257, 132

Revocation of POA, 184, 120-122

Right-to-Die, 88-89, 96-97

S

Springing POA, 207, 169, 81, 155, 298

State laws, 185-187, 189, 34, 165-166, 122, 125-126, 149-150, 157-158, 162, 299, 27-29

Statutory forms, 185-186, 34, 166, 44-45, 83, 150-153, 155, 158, 160-161

Surrogate, 226-227, 239, 241-242, 33, 48, 64, 84, 93, 96, 155, 298

T

Terminal condition, 224-225, 229, 238-241, 249-250, 103, 123, 298

Terri Schiavo, 306, 91, 95-96

U

Uniform Determination of Death Act, 98

Uniform Health-Care Decisions Act, 162

Uniform Power of Attorney Act, 45, 151

Unlimited POA, 45, 79, 81-82

V

Ventilator, 304-305, 90, 108, 111-112